BUILDING
SCHOOL-COMMUNITY
PARTNERSHIPS

BUILDING SCHOOL-COMMUNITY PARTNERSHIPS

Collaboration for Student Success

MAVIS G. SANDERS

Foreword by Joyce L. Epstein

CORWIN PRESS
A SAGE Publications Company
Thousand Oaks, California

For information:

Corwin Press
A Sage Publications Company
2455 Teller Road
Thousand Oaks, California 91320
www.corwinpress.com

Sage Publications Ltd.
1 Oliver's Yard
55 City Road
London EC1Y 1SP
United Kingdom

Sage Publications India Pvt. Ltd.
B-42, Panchsheel Enclave
Post Box 4109
New Delhi 110 017 India

Printed in the United States of America

Library of Congress Cataloging-in-Publication Data

Sanders, Mavis G.
Building school-community partnerships: Collaboration for student success / Mavis G. Sanders.
    p. cm.
Includes bibliographical references and index.
ISBN 1-4129-1764-6 (cloth)—ISBN 1-4129-1765-4 (pbk.)
    1. Community and school—United States. 2. Academic achievement—United States. I. Title.
LC221.S26 2006
371.19—dc22   2005014772

This book is printed on acid-free paper.

05   06   07   08   09   10   9   8   7   6   5   4   3   2   1

Acquisitions Editor:	Elizabeth Brenkus
Editorial Assistants:	Candice L. Ling and Desirée Enayati
Production Editor:	Laureen Shea
Copy Editor:	Marilyn Power Scott
Typesetter:	C&M Digitals (P) Ltd.
Proofreader:	Kristin Bergstad
Indexer:	Judy Hunt
Cover Designer:	Rose Storey
Graphic Designer:	Scott Van Atta

Contents

Foreword   ix
  Joyce L. Epstein

Preface   xi

Acknowledgments   xv

About the Author   xvii

1. Community Involvement: Why and What?   1
   Rationales for Community Involvement in Schools   1
   Community Involvement in Schools: Form and Fashion   3
   Obstacles to Community Partnerships   8
   Summary   13

2. A Closer Look at Common Community Partnerships   14
   Business Partnerships   14
   University Partnerships   16
   Service Learning Partnerships   18
   School-Linked Service Integration   20
   Faith-Based Partnerships   22
   Summary   25

3. Components of Successful Community Partnerships   28
   High-Functioning Schools   28
   Student-Centered Learning Environments   30
   Effective Partnership Teams   31
   Principal Leadership   33
   External Support   36
   Summary   38

**4. Building Capacity for Successful Community
   Partnerships: A Vignette**   39
   The School   39
   The Goal   40
   The Team   40

The Project 41
The Community Partners 41
The Results 42
Lessons Learned 43
Summary 45

5. Bringing the Community In: An Elementary School Story **47**
Background 47
Community Partners 48
Commitment to Students' Learning 51
Principal Leadership 54
Action Team for Partnerships 56
Welcoming School Climate 57
Two-Way Communication 58
Summary 60

6. Creating Closer Community Ties: A High School Study **62**
Background 62
Principal Leadership 66
A Student Focus 66
Community Partners and Activities 67
Summary 71

7. Promising Practices for Community Partnerships **73**
Activity 1: Goal—Improve Reading (2004) 74
Activity 2: Goal—Improve Math Skills (2003) 74
Activity 3: Goal—Increase Students'
 Awareness of Career Opportunities (2001) 75
Activity 4: Goal—Improve Ninth-Grade Performance
 on State Proficiency Exam (2002) 76
Activity 5: Goal—Improve Student Writing
 and Technology Skills (2002) 77
Activity 6: Goal—Improve Student Reading (2002) 78
Activity 7: Goal—Improve School Landscaping (2002) 79
Activity 8: Goal—Provide Community Service (2002) 79
Activity 9: Goal—Improve Student Oral and Written
 Communication (2004) 81
Activity 10: Goal—Improve Facilities for
 Students With Disabilities (2004) 82
Activity 11: Goal—Improve Student
 Science Skills (2000) 82
Activity 12: Goal—Provide Afterschool
 Activities for Middle School Students (2000) 83
Summary 84

8. **Preparing Educational Leaders for Community Partnerships: A Workshop Agenda**   **85**

    Building Community Partnerships Agenda   86

    Summary   89

9. **Concluding Thoughts**   **102**

Resource A: Sample Activities   **104**

    Activity 1: Locating Community Partners   105

    Activity 2: Improving the Partnership Process   106

    Activity 3: Improving Community Partnership Quality   107

    Activity 4: Garnering Principal Support for Partnerships   108

Resource B: Sample Letters   **109**

    Sample Letter 1: Partnership Communication   110

    Sample Letter 2: Partnership Activity Follow-Up   111

Endnotes   **112**

References   **114**

Index   **121**

Foreword

Many schools working to improve their programs of family and community involvement are struggling to find meaningful community partners. They puzzle, Where *is* our community? Is it around the school? Where students live? Where families work or worship? What are the community's interests in our students' success? Educators also wonder, How can we make sure that our community partners work with us collaboratively, not contentiously, to help improve the school program and increase students' success?

In *Building School-Community Partnerships: Collaboration for Student Success,* Mavis G. Sanders addresses these and other questions with excellent information, examples, and advice. She explains clearly how to include school-community connections (e.g., businesses, cultural groups, senior citizens, faith-based organizations, universities, and other partners) in comprehensive programs of school, family, and community partnerships.

Sanders has conducted groundbreaking research for over a decade, delving deeply into ways that elementary, middle, and high schools work successfully with community partners, resolve challenges, and sustain collaborations. She developed a complete catalog of community partners and identified an array of school-community activities that strengthen families, expand students' learning experiences, and improve school programs and curricula.

Because most research on partnerships has focused on schools and families, this book on school-community connections is a welcome and timely resource for researchers, school and district leaders, and teams of school-based educators, parents, and community partners who work together to develop and improve their programs of school, family, and community partnerships. Sanders' work—sharp, insightful, and comprehensive—will guide future research and help schools and school districts improve their partnership programs.

—Joyce L. Epstein, PhD

Director, Center on School, Family and Community Partnerships
and the National Network of Partnership Schools

Johns Hopkins University, Baltimore, Maryland

Preface

Teachers often find themselves using their personal incomes to purchase needed classroom materials for their students or inundated with tasks that could be accomplished by school volunteers. Parents are often less than satisfied with school equipment and materials or eager to find ways to support their children's nonacademic interests. Principals struggle to find ways to fund school events or improve school-based professional development; and far too many students suffer from a lack of extended learning opportunities. Most K–12 educators can add to these examples and attest to the frustration and constraints in teaching and learning created by a lack of resources.

Resources, then, both human and material, are at the center of educational excellence. Community involvement is one way to generate resources that are essential for effective schooling. When such resources are appropriately channeled, they can support innovative educational programs that meet the learning needs of increasingly diverse student populations and promote equity in the educational opportunities available to all students.

Here, *community involvement* is defined as connections between schools and community individuals, organizations, and businesses that are forged to directly or indirectly promote students' social, emotional, physical, and intellectual development.[1] Community within this definition of school-community partnerships is not constrained by the geographic boundaries of neighborhoods, but refers more to the "interactions that can occur within or transcend local boundaries" (Nettles, 1991, p. 380).[2] While parent involvement can be included within the broader definition of community involvement, it is important to note that parent involvement is not a central focus of this book.

As described in Chapter 1, however, community involvement activities can be developed to assist families in supporting their children's learning and school engagement. Furthermore, parental support can help schools to identify, attract, and maintain community connections. Schools are, thus, encouraged to think of community involvement and parent involvement as two sides of the same coin in their school improvement efforts, and to explore resources that currently exist to help schools develop and improve their outreach to parents.[3]

This book is a result of five years of research and teaching in the area of school-community partnerships.[4] The research included surveys of hundreds of school leaders and case studies of elementary, middle, and high schools in rural, suburban, and urban areas in the United States. At the time the studies were conducted, participating schools were members of the National Network of Partnership Schools (NNPS).[5] NNPS was begun in 1996 to provide research-based support, guidance, and tools to schools, districts, and states seeking to achieve or maintain high levels of family and community engagement. The educators that have been involved in NNPS activities have been essential in generating new knowledge on the processes and outcomes of school, family, and community partnerships. I am indebted to them and my colleagues at NNPS for their hard work and cooperation over the years. Although I do not include a separate methods section in the book, when relevant, I refer to the studies on which individual chapters are based.

The book is written to serve as a resource for educational leaders who seek to establish school-community partnerships to achieve goals for their schools and the students, families, and communities they serve. It is organized in eight chapters that when taken together offer a broad and practical overview of theory, research, and practice in the field.

Chapter 1 provides background information on community partnerships. It describes why such partnerships are important; how they can be organized to focus on students, families, schools, and communities; and a variety of community partners with whom schools can collaborate. It also details several obstacles schools face in developing and maintaining effective community partnerships and strategies to address these obstacles.

Chapter 2 provides in-depth information on five prevalent kinds of school-community partnerships; they are defined by the primary community partners involved: (a) businesses, (b) universities, (c) organizations that provide internships for youth, (d) service agencies and professionals, and (e) faith-based organizations. I review the conceptual and empirical literature that has been generated on each type of partnership. The review highlights key factors that influence school-community collaboration with these and other partners.

Chapter 3 presents a model that outlines essential components for the successful implementation of school-community partnerships. These components are (a) a high-functioning school, (b) a student-centered environment, (c) an effective partnership team, (d) principal leadership, and (e) external support. When present, these components help schools to attract and maintain a variety of desirable community partners to achieve specified goals and overcome the common obstacles to effective partnership program development discussed in Chapter 1. Drawing from the efforts of one teacher-leader, Chapter 4 discusses how educators, through incremental, focused steps, can build their schools' capacity for successful community partnerships.

Chapters 5 and 6 include case studies that exemplify how the components described in Chapter 3 work in practice. Community partnerships at an urban elementary and rural high school, respectively, are described. These cases show how K–12 schools with different needs, goals, and student populations can develop community linkages that support school improvement and enhance students' learning.

Chapter 7 offers several examples of school-community partnership activities being conducted in schools throughout the United States. These examples are taken from activities published in NNPS's annual collection of Promising Partnership Practices. Selected activities further illustrate the wide variety of partnership activities that can help schools achieve important goals for students' success.

Finally, Chapter 8 provides materials that educators can use to conduct professional development workshops on school, family, and community partnerships. A sample agenda is provided, along with small-group and whole-group exercises and materials that can be used as overheads or handouts or adapted for PowerPoint presentations.

The concluding section describes additional resources that will be helpful to readers who would like to further explore key aspects of school, family, and community partnerships. It is followed by Resource A, which includes exercises to help teams that are just beginning the partnership process or are interested in improving the quality of their current partnerships. Resource B includes sample letters that readers can use to communicate annually with community partners.

The current reform era of high-stakes testing and accountability, alongside shrinking educational budgets, demands that schools seek bold and innovative ways to build strong learning environments for all students. Goal-oriented school-community partnerships are one way to do so. Educators can and should be in the forefront of creating opportunities for such partnerships. The resources generated can help to produce the kinds of schools that all children and youth deserve.

Acknowledgments

S pecial thanks are due to the staff of the National Network of Partnership Schools; its Director, Joyce L. Epstein, a pioneer in the field of school, family, and community partnerships; and Natalie Rodriguez Jansorn, Karen Clark Salinas, Steven B. Sheldon, and Kenyatta Williams. They have individually and collectively taught me so much about this important work. Thanks also are due to members of NNPS who give school, family, and partnerships life in their daily work in schools, districts, and state departments of education. I am especially thankful to those school leaders who, with generosity and enthusiasm, have allowed me and my colleagues to share their successes, challenges, and insights with others. Thanks also are due to students in my courses on school, family, and community partnerships. Our interaction has broadened and deepened my understanding of the process and place of partnerships in educational practice.

I also am indebted to Corwin Press, especially to Elizabeth Brenkus, Candice Ling, and Marilyn Power Scott, for their assistance in making the idea of this book a reality. I am grateful to my colleague and dear friend, Antoinette Mitchell, for reviewing early drafts of the manuscript and providing unwavering support and encouragement for any and every undertaking. Last, I am especially grateful to my parents, Grover and Vera Sanders, and my sisters Desiree, Vetta, Pamela, and Camilla who provide endless encouragement and an invaluable sense of community.

Corwin Press gratefully acknowledges the contributions of the following individuals:

Julie Boyd, Principal
Ashburn Elementary School
Ashburn, VA

Diane Dorfman, Research Associate
Northwest Regional Educational Laboratory
Portland, OR

Nora Friedman, Principal
South Grove Elementary School
Syosset, NY

Dolores Gribouski, Principal
Columbus Park School
Worcester, MA

Benjamin Ngwudike, Assistant Professor
Jackson State University
Jackson, MS

Barry Stark, Principal
Norris Middle School
Firth, NE

Paul Young, Corwin Author, Executive Director
West After School Center
Lancaster, OH

About the Author

Mavis G. Sanders, PhD in education from Stanford University, holds a joint appointment as research scientist at the Center for Research on the Education of Students Placed at Risk and associate professor in the Graduate Division of Education at Johns Hopkins University. She has published and presented numerous papers on the processes and outcomes of school, family, and community connections, including articles appearing in *Urban Education*, *Journal of Negro Education*, *Educational Leadership*, and the *Elementary School Journal*. She is coauthor of *School, Family, and Community Partnerships: Your Handbook for Action*, which provides tools and information to assist schools, districts, and state departments of education to plan and implement programs of partnership. A recent book, *Schooling Students Placed at Risk: Research, Policy, and Practice in the Education of Poor and Minority Adolescents*, includes several chapters that highlight the importance of family and community involvement for the school success of all students. Her research and teaching interests include school reform, parent and community involvement, and African American student achievement.

This book is dedicated to my husband, Jeffrey,
to whom I turn for support, and our children,
Shori Vera and Jeffrey Ojia, to whom I turn for inspiration.

1 Community Involvement

Why and What?

The notion that the community has a role to play in the education of youth is long standing in the United States. From Dewey's concept of community schools at the turn of the twentieth century to calls for community control from parents and community activists in the late 1960s, community involvement has been a central theme in educational reform. Today, community involvement has taken on renewed significance in configurations and discussions of school improvement. Federal, state, and local educational legislation; political slogans; professional addresses; and casual conversations about schooling are likely to include references to the role or responsibility of the community. Why has community involvement had such longevity in educational reform and discourse? I see four compelling reasons, described in the following discussion.

RATIONALES FOR COMMUNITY INVOLVEMENT IN SCHOOLS

Within the theoretical and conceptual literature, a number of rationales for community involvement in schools exist. Proponents of such involvement emphasize its importance for effective school functioning, economic competitiveness, student well-being, and community health and development. When describing the importance of community involvement for effective school functioning, proponents most often focus on the mounting responsibilities placed on schools by a nation with children and youth who are increasingly placed "at risk." According to Shore (1994),

> Too many schools and school systems are failing to carry out their
> basic educational mission. Many of them—both in urban and rural
> settings—are overwhelmed by the social and emotional needs of
> children who are growing up in poverty. (p. 2)

Proponents argue that schools need additional resources to successfully
educate all students and that these resources, both human and material, are
housed in students' communities (Epstein, 1995; Melaville, 1998; Waddock,
1995). They contend that the traditional isolated way that many schools have
functioned is anachronistic in a time of changing family demographics, an
increasingly demanding workplace, and growing student diversity (Ascher,
1988; Crowson & Boyd, 1993; Heath & McLaughlin, 1987, 1996; Kirst &
McLaughlin, 1990). Ascher (1988), for example, called for an expanded
vision of those who should participate in the task of educating our nation's
students. This vision calls for schools that are open to involvement by the
local and wider community and that are responsive to community needs.

Arguments for community involvement to improve school functioning are closely linked to those that emphasize the importance of community
involvement for U.S. economic competitiveness. Proponents of this view
argue that a primary responsibility of schools is to prepare the nation's workforce. A well-educated workforce is seen as vital to economic productivity
and expansion. This view of the role of schools is generally accepted in the
United States and has been central to national educational legislation and
policy for decades.

Community involvement is seen as one way to help schools produce
a more capable workforce. According to proponents of this view, jobs in
the twenty-first century exist in increasingly complicated environments and
require workers who are competent beyond a basic skills level. Students need
advanced language, technical, and communication skills to succeed in the
kinds of jobs that are currently available. Proponents argue that school-
community partnerships, specifically those that involve businesses, are criti-
cally important because business leaders, managers, and personnel are
uniquely equipped to help schools prepare students for the changing workplace
(Fitzgerald, 1997; Hopkins & Wendel, 1997; Nasworthy & Rood, 1990).

Merz and Furman (1997) described this reform perspective as
gesellschaftlich in nature because the schooling process is viewed from an
instrumental perspective. That is, schools are seen primarily as a means to
serve national economic interests by preparing students for the workplace.
They contrast this perspective with gemeinschaft reform values that emphasize relationships, interpersonal connections, and providing students with a
sense of purpose and belonging in society. For many of its proponents, community involvement is seen as one way to restore gemeinschaft values to the

schooling process. These values are viewed as fundamental to creating schools that nurture the well-being of children and youth.

Proponents of community involvement for student well-being argue that because of changes in the structure and function of U.S. families and neighborhoods, many children and youth, regardless of socioeconomic background, are growing up without the social capital necessary for their healthy development. Social capital is created and exchanged through positive, caring relationships in which knowledge, guidance, and values are shared (Coleman, 1987, 1988). Proponents of community involvement for student well-being argue that schools can increase students' social capital through their connections with students' communities (Benson, 1996; McLaughlin, Irby, & Langman, 1994; Toffler & Toffler, 1995). They contend that through a variety of community volunteer and service integration programs, schools can become islands of hope for students whose social environments are increasingly stressed and fragmented (Dryfoos, 1998, 2002, 2003; Nettles, 1991).

Finally, some proponents argue that community involvement in schools is important for building and maintaining healthy communities. When discussing the role of school-community collaborations in rural communities, Combs and Bailey (1992) argued that as often the largest and most visible institutions, schools should be involved in rural economic development. They contended that the educational, social, and recreational needs of the adult rural population can be enhanced by utilizing local school facilities and expertise. In turn, they argued, schools can use the community as a learning resource.

Keith (1996) similarly argued for a new conceptualization of community involvement in schools. She argued that schools should develop horizontal ties with the community to foster the "social networks, educational, and economic opportunities and cultural richness" (p. 254) that is central to social and economic growth. Benson (1996) also suggested that community development should be a goal of school-community collaborations, because such collaborations require healthy communities in order to be successful in serving youth. Benson defines healthy communities as those that have not only strong socioeconomic and service infrastructures but also are rich in social capital.

COMMUNITY INVOLVEMENT IN SCHOOLS: FORM AND FASHION

Community Partnership Foci

The different rationales for community involvement can be realized through a variety of partnership activities. School-community partnerships can be student centered, family centered, school centered, community centered, or any combination of these. Student-centered activities include those that provide direct services or goods to students: for example, student awards and incentives, scholarships, tutoring and mentoring programs, afterschool enrichment programs, and job shadowing and other career-focused activities. Family-centered activities are those that have parents or entire families as their primary focus. This category includes activities such as parenting workshops, GED and other adult education classes, family incentives and awards, family counseling, and family fun and learning nights. School-centered activities are those that benefit the school as a whole, such as beautification projects or the donation of school equipment and materials, or activities that benefit the faculty, such as staff development and classroom assistance. Community-centered activities have as their primary focus the community and its citizens: for example, charitable outreach, art and science exhibits in community venues, and community revitalization and beautification projects (see Table 1.1).

Survey research of 443 school members of the National Network of Partnership Schools (NNPS) in 1998[5] revealed much about the focus of schools' partnership efforts. Overall, most schools reported that their community partnership activities were student centered. This finding suggests that schools may focus their partnership activities too narrowly. Schools may not have fully explored collaborative activities to benefit the total school program or to assist in providing adults in students' families with primary services, skills training, or other parental supports. Such school-centered and

Table 1.1   Foci of Partnership Activities

Activity Focus	Sample Activities
Student-centered	Student awards, student incentives, scholarships, student trips, tutors, mentors, job shadowing, and other services and products for students
Family-centered	Parent workshops, family fun nights, GED and other adult education classes, parent incentives and rewards, counseling and other forms of assistance
School-centered	Equipment and materials, beautification and repair, teacher incentives and awards, funds for school events and programs, office and classroom assistance
Community-centered	Community beautification, student exhibits and performances, charity and other outreach

SOURCE: Adapted from Sanders (2001).

family-centered partnership activities might be especially important for high-need, resource-poor schools.

The community-centered category was the least represented of the four, indicating that many schools had not developed partnership activities that served the larger community. Developing two-way or reciprocal school-community partnership activities is a key challenge for schools as they work to improve and expand their programs of school, family, and community partnership (Epstein et al., 2002). Through community-focused activities, schools, families, and students can contribute to the larger community and serve as catalysts for community action and development.

Potential Community Partners

Schools can collaborate with a variety of community partners to plan and implement partnership activities. The survey of NNPS schools helped to generate the categories of partners identified in Table 1.2. These partners include (a) large corporations and small businesses, (b) universities and educational institutions, (c) government and military agencies, (d) health care organizations, (e) faith-based organizations, (f) national service and volunteer organizations, (g) senior citizen organizations, (h) cultural and recreational institutions, (i) media organizations, (j) sports franchises and associations, (k) other groups such as fraternities and sororities, and (l) community volunteers that can provide resources and social support to youth and schools (see Table 1.2).

The over 400 NNPS school members surveyed reported 817 school-community partnership activities. Of these, the greatest proportion (366 or 45%) involved one or more business partners. These included small and large local businesses, such as bakeries, groceries, barbershops, funeral homes, beauty salons, banks, utility companies, and florists, as well as national corporations and franchises, such as LensCrafters, IBM, State Farm Insurance, General Motors, Wal-Mart, AT&T, Pizza Hut, Burger King, and McDonald's.

Seventy-seven (9%) of the reported activities included universities, colleges, and other educational institutions, including neighboring schools. Health care organizations, including hospitals, mental health facilities, and health foundations, were involved in 68 (8%), while government and military agencies were partners in 62 (8%) of the activities. Examples of government and military agencies include fire and police departments, chambers of commerce, and other state and local agencies and departments.

National service and volunteer organizations, including Rotary Club, Lions Club, AmeriCorps, Concerned Black Men, Inc., the Urban League,

Table 1.2   Potential Partners for School-Community Collaboration

Community Partners

Businesses/Corporations (e.g., local businesses, national corporations and franchises)

Educational Institutions (e.g., colleges and universities, high schools, and other educational institutions)

Health Care Organizations (e.g., hospitals, health care centers, mental health facilities, health departments, health foundations, and associations)

Government and Military Agencies (e.g., fire departments, police departments, chambers of commerce, city councils, other local and state government agencies and departments)

National Service and Volunteer Organizations (e.g., Rotary Club, Lions Club, Kiwanis Club, VISTA, Concerned Black Men, Inc., Shriners, Boy & Girl Scouts, YMCA, United Way, AmeriCorps, Urban League)

Faith-Based Organizations (e.g., churches, mosques, synagogues, other religious organizations, and charities)

Senior Citizens Organizations (e.g., nursing homes, senior volunteer and service organizations)

Cultural and Recreational Institutions (e.g., zoos, museums, libraries, recreational centers)

Media Organizations (e.g., local newspapers, radio stations, cable networks)

Sports Franchises and Associations (e.g., minor and major league sports teams, NBA, NCAA)

Other Community Organizations (e.g., fraternities, sororities, foundations, neighborhood associations, political organizations, alumni)

Community Individuals (e.g., individual volunteers from the surrounding school community)

SOURCE: Adapted from Sanders (2001).

and Boys and Girls Clubs, were involved in 49 (6%) of the partnership activities described by schools in the National Network. Faith organizations, such as churches, synagogues, and religious charities, participated in 47 (6%) of the reported activities. Senior citizens organizations were involved in 25 (3%) of the 817 activities reported. Zoos, libraries, recreational centers, museums, and other cultural and recreational institutions participated in 20 (2%) of the activities.

Media organizations and sports franchises also were represented, albeit in smaller numbers. Other community-based organizations, including sororities and fraternities, alumni organizations, neighborhood associations, and local service organizations, were involved in 79 (10%) of the activities. Nineteen (2%) of them included individuals in the school community volunteering their time, energy, and talents.

As described, schools in the sample relied heavily on businesses and corporations as their partners. Schools' preference for business partners may be due to their greater visibility, availability, and familiarity. However, this reliance may result in schools underutilizing other community partners who also may provide goods and services to their faculties, students, and families. For example, there were noticeably few cultural and recreational institutions among the many partners reported. Similarly, activities that included faith-based organizations, media organizations, and national service and volunteer organizations were limited. These findings suggest that schools may need to broaden their definition of "community," and reach out to organizations that are less visible than businesses but are equally interested in partnering with schools.

Survey data also suggest that schools may currently not make the most of their community partnerships. For example, most partnership activities with senior citizens' organizations involved students visiting senior citizens' facilities. Few partnership activities gave senior citizens opportunities to provide services and information to schools, families, and students. In addition to broadening their definitions of "community," then, schools also need to expand their visions of how community partners can help them to facilitate school improvement and students' success.

Range of Complexity in Community Partnerships

The kinds of community partnerships that schools implement can vary in complexity. If viewed on a continuum, simple partnerships on the far left end are characterized by short-term exchanges of goods or services (see Fig. 1.1). Such partnerships require very little coordination, planning, or cultural and structural shifts in school functioning. Thus they are relatively easy to implement, especially for schools that may lack the experience needed for more complex partnerships. When well implemented, their impact is likely to be positive, albeit limited.

Community partnership activities increase in complexity as you move along the continuum. Activities located in the middle of the continuum might include a partnership between an elementary school and a local library to provide a series of parent workshops on supporting children's literacy development at a variety of community sites. This partnership activity may require several meetings over time to identify appropriate topics, materials, and venues as well as to plan, schedule, publicize, and evaluate the events.

Figure 1.1	Community Partnerships: Range of Complexity

Simple Partnerships	Complex Partnerships
• Short term	• Long term
• Unidirectional exchange	• Bidirectional or multidirectional exchange
• Low level of interaction	• High level of interaction
• Limited planning	• Extensive planning and coordination
(e.g., incentives for awards programs, donation of school materials/supplies)	(e.g., full-service community schools, professional development schools)

On the far right end of the continuum, activities are long term and characterized by bidirectional or multidirectional exchange, high levels of interaction, and extensive planning and coordination (see Fig. 1.1). For example, community resources and supports can be integrated with educational services in the form of full-service community schools. Several variations of community schools exist. These include (a) school-based health clinics, facilities that provide health counseling, education, and services in school buildings operated by outside health agencies; (b) school-based youth centers that provide afterschool, recreational, mentoring, employment, and other needed services to students in extended day programs; and (c) family resource centers, facilities located in schools where parents can receive supports and services such as employment assistance, immigration information, food, clothing, counseling, and early child care (Dryfoos, 1998). As described in Chapter 2, partnerships as complex as school-based integrated services may require additional personnel, hired to coordinate and oversee program implementation and evaluation.

OBSTACLES TO COMMUNITY PARTNERSHIPS

A number of obstacles to school-community partnerships exist; some may be more prevalent at some schools than others. Schools must address these obstacles before they can maximize the benefits of their connections with community members, businesses, and organizations.

Cushing and Kohl (1997) identified three barriers to successful school-community collaborations: (a) fear of public scrutiny, (b) staff burnout, and (c) teachers' and administrators' negative perceptions of students' families and communities. Mawhinney (1994) and Epstein (1995) also identified barriers to effective collaborations with the community. According to these authors, one of the most pervasive hindrances to collaboration is territorialism or, as Crowson and Boyd (1993, p. 152) noted, "unresolved issues of information sharing, resource mingling and professional turf."

The survey data gathered from 443 NNPS school members highlighted additional barriers to the successful implementation of school-community partnerships. When asked what obstacles they faced in developing and expanding their community partnership activities, 233 schools responded. Only 18% of these respondents reported that they faced no obstacles in planning and implementing partnership activities. Most reported several obstacles, including insufficient participation, time, community resources, leadership, funding, communication, and focus. In this section, I briefly discuss these obstacles and recommended strategies to address them.

Participation

Nearly one third (30%) of respondents who reported challenges identified insufficient participation as an obstacle to school-community partnerships. Similar to findings reported by Cushing and Kohl (1997), some respondents noted that involving school faculty was a challenge. However, others reported that involving families, students, and community members also was a problem as the following responses illustrate.

> We (the ATP) asked teachers to each contact two businesses for a Book Plate Drive, they all refused. . . . Teachers feel they do enough (School 29).

> Since our district is so spread out, we have a difficult time getting people to go to different community activities (School 474).

> Our reading program got off to a very slow start. We had difficulty getting community members to volunteer to assist our youngsters (School 195).

Several survey respondents identified strategies to improve participation in school-community activities. Some suggested reaching out beyond faculty members to volunteers for help in coordinating partnership activities. Some suggested using local media and school newsletters to increase awareness of activities. Still others mentioned making reminder phone calls, encouraging participants to bring friends to activities, and providing door prizes and other incentives for participation. Other strategies included changing the time of activities to accommodate more interested individuals; organizing Saturday as well as weekday functions; providing transportation, food, and babysitting services; and using community facilities for activities.

Lack of Time

A second and perhaps related obstacle was that of insufficient time. Nearly one quarter (24%) of school respondents reported that they found it difficult to find time to meet, identify, and contact potential community partners and to implement partnership activities. According to these respondents,

> Our big challenge is having time to approach businesses in the area (School 93).

> It is difficult finding time to create more partnerships or different ones (School 101).

> We need more time to contact organizations and encourage their involvement. We also need time for staff to work with agencies and parents (School 124).

> Time is a challenge. The time that the Downtown Merchant's Association can meet (between 8:30–9:15) is when we are teaching (School 133).

Respondents offered several strategies to address the time limitations many schools faced. They suggested that schools identify a wider range of staff and parent and community volunteers to plan and implement activities. Some respondents also suggested that schools utilize a team approach so that the tasks of planning, implementing, and evaluating partnership activities can be shared among its members. Furthermore, the respondents suggested that school-based teams do their planning in the spring or summer of each school year so that they are ready to implement activities in the fall.

Community Resources

About 12% of respondents reported identifying community partners as a primary obstacle to school-community partnerships. Some of these respondents noted that they were located in resource-poor communities with few businesses and other community-based organizations. Others reported that competition from other schools made finding partners difficult, and still others indicated that their students were bussed to the school, which made community partners difficult to identify. The respondents explained,

> We are in competition with 12 other schools seeking partnerships with businesses in our community (School 95).

> Our challenge is limited business/industry to draw on (School 330).

Ours is a small, rural area that is in an economically distressed area. Community partners are difficult to find (School 475).

To address the obstacle of limited community resources, some respondents encouraged schools to identify community partners other than businesses and corporations. Table 1.2 is a resource that schools can use to consider other potential partners. Respondents also noted that schools can learn more about available community resources by attending local community events and meetings, including those of their local chambers of commerce. Other respondents emphasized the importance of schools networking with individuals within and outside their immediate geographic area to secure partners.

Leadership

Some respondents (8%) found that inadequate leadership was an obstacle. They reported that without an individual or individuals to lead in the development, evaluation, and maintenance of school-community partnership activities, coordinating and sustaining such activities was challenging. Typical responses were

We need leadership within the school to develop the necessary relationships (School 336).

We need a coordinator to work with the Rotary Club and the school (School 259).

Our biggest challenge is time and consistent leadership (School 667).

The most frequently reported strategy to address insufficient leadership was to involve other school groups, like the school leadership council or Parent-Teacher Association (PTA), in the planning and implementation of school-community partnerships. School respondents also suggested building a wide and diverse pool of leaders by providing training on school, family, and community partnerships to the entire school staff, as well as interested parents and community members.

Funding

Some respondents (8%) also viewed funding as an obstacle. They stated,

We need an operating budget (School 72).

Lack of funds was our biggest challenge (School 107).

Finding the funds needed to provide materials, trips, speakers, and/or incentives is difficult (School 45).

Many respondents suggested using PTA, PTO, 21st Century Learning Communities, Safe and Drug Free Schools, or Title 1 funds; soliciting donations from businesses; and holding fundraisers. Others suggested applying for small and large grants to secure funding for partnership activities. Parent and community coordinators in some district and state offices and departments of education offer such grants. In addition, excellent Web sites for finding grant-making organizations to support school-based activities include *The Center for Education Reform*, http://www.edreform.com/info/grant.htm, and *Grants for NonProfits: Education*, http://www.lib.msu.edu/harris23/grants/2educat.htm. Other respondents noted that community partners themselves may offset some of the costs associated with partnership activities through the provision of goods and services.

Communication

A small percentage (6%) of respondents identified communication as a challenge. Some schools faced this obstacle because of the linguistic diversity of their student and family populations. Others found it difficult to communicate in a timely manner to increase participation in activities. Schools reported,

We found that the language barrier between many families and English-speaking community members was a challenge (School 231).

Parent attendance at community activities was poor due to the lack of communication (School 162).

To improve communication, some school respondents suggested using students to make reminder phone calls; using interpreters to translate written notices and information provided at school-community activities and meetings; and using a variety of communication sources—for example, newsletters, newspapers, television, and radio—to convey information about partnership opportunities and activities.

Focus

A few respondents (3%) also identified insufficient focus as an obstacle. That so few respondents identified this area as an obstacle may reflect the current use of site-based management and school improvement plans that identify school goals and foci for the academic year. In fact, the primary strategy offered to improve the focus of schools' community partnership activities was to link the activities to school improvement goals.

SUMMARY

Community involvement can equip schools to provide students with more relevant, challenging learning opportunities in nurturing environments. Schools can collaborate with a variety of community partners. This chapter identified twelve categories of community partners to help educational leaders think about the "community" more broadly. What is most important in partner selection, however, is that schools identify community partners and develop partnership activities that will help them to achieve goals that support students' learning and school improvement efforts. Partnerships for partnerships' sake will not help a school achieve and maintain excellence.

School-community partnerships can be long- or short-term; their activities can be student-, family-, community-, or school-focused; and they can require limited or extensive planning. Schools with little or no experience in planning and implementing school-community partnerships should begin with simple activities. As their experience and capacity grow, schools can incorporate increasingly more complex community partnerships as need dictates and opportunity allows. No two schools are exactly alike. The array of community partnerships that each school ultimately achieves, therefore, will be different and should reflect its goals for students' learning and success.

School-community partnerships are not without obstacles. Reported obstacles include insufficient funding; time; and faculty, parent, and community participation. This chapter recommends several strategies that school leaders can implement to address obstacles that commonly arise when developing school-community partnerships. In order to do so, however, they first need to understand factors that can create and exacerbate barriers to successful implementation. These are highlighted in Chapter 2, which looks closely at partnerships between schools and five common community partners: (a) businesses, (b) universities, (c) organizations that provide internships for youth, (d) service agencies and professionals, and (e) faith-based institutions.

2

A Closer Look at Common Community Partnerships

As described in Chapter 1, schools can collaborate with a wide variety of community partners to obtain the material and human resources they need to achieve important goals for students' learning. Some of these partners are more prevalent than others and have been studied in greater depth. In this chapter, I discuss the literature that has been generated on school-community collaborations that involve five common partners. This discussion provides a closer look into the ways in which such partnerships are coordinated and factors that influence their effectiveness. The chapter ends with five questions that school leaders should consider before collaborating with these or other community agencies and organizations.

BUSINESS PARTNERSHIPS

The most common school-community linkages are partnerships with businesses and corporations, which can be involved in education in a variety of ways. Mickelson (1999) has identified six types of corporate involvement. The first two types include large corporations that exert their financial and symbolic influence nationally through large-scale empirical studies, or material support for systemic reform efforts (e.g., Ford Foundation). Type 3 involvement includes midlevel corporate actors who influence state and local educational reform through participation on high profile task forces. Type 4 is the most common form, in which corporate employees participate in educational programs and activities at school sites as mentors, tutors, guest speakers, and in other ways. In Type 5 corporate involvement, business leaders serve as educational decision makers, most noticeably on local school boards. Finally, Type 6 includes for-profit companies that sell their products or services as systemic reforms (e.g., Edison Project).

Over the past decade, school-business partnerships of all types have significantly increased and are generally characterized as beneficial for students, families, communities, schools and the businesses themselves (Bucy, 1990; Engeln, 2003; Families and Work Institute, 1995; Partnership for Family Involvement, 1997; U.S. Department of Education, 1994). Such partnerships can provide funding for school projects, tutors, internships, incentives, and a host of other supports for schools and students. Recent case studies, however, show that the positive effects of school-business partnerships are not guaranteed. Their success is largely determined by how thoughtfully they are planned and with whose input.

For example, Mickelson (1999) conducted a case study of two school-business partnerships in Charlotte, North Carolina. The first was a $2 million grant to fund the creation of a complex of four technology-rich schools adjacent to an IBM facility. The second was a collaboration between IBM and the Charlotte-Mecklenburg Education Foundation designed to bring computer and technology specialists into ten of the district's twenty-two middle schools that did not have magnet programs. The first project resulted in the development of technology-rich schools, but it was mired in controversy over questions of financing and student enrollment. The impact of the second project was significantly compromised because the volunteer technology specialists were not appropriately trained and prepared to be of service in the schools, nor were the schools prepared for the technology provided.

Neither initiative included school personnel, students' parents, or community members in the planning and development of the partnerships. This top-down approach reduced the likelihood of successful implementation or significant, long-term influence on the school reform process. A case study of business partnerships in the Houston school district yielded similar findings. According to Longoria (1998), by 1993 there were approximately thirty community-business-education coalitions in Houston, most dominated by business sector advocacy. Largely as a result of this advocacy, 2,322 individual school-business partnerships were implemented in 1994. Most of these partnerships were focused on school improvement and student achievement. Partnership activities included providing mentors for individual students, donating school equipment, and funding awards for improved student attendance.

Despite increases in student test scores on the Texas Assessment of Academic Skills and the Scholastic Aptitude Test subsequent to the business sector's involvement, Longoria (1998) raised several concerns about the elite-driven and entrepreneurial style of business involvement in Houston schools. Central among these was the concern that the involvement occurred without meaningful input from teachers, administrators, parents, and community activists. He argued that the exclusion of these key stakeholders created tensions that might, in the future, undermine the benefits of the partnerships.

Nasworthy and Rood (1990) also underscored the importance of including key stakeholders, especially school administrators and faculty, in the development of school-business partnerships. The authors identified three strategies to foster successful partnership practices. These strategies also are advocated in the *Guiding Principles for Business and School Partnerships* developed by the Council for Corporate and School Partnerships (see Engeln, 2003).

First, the school administration should be involved in the decision to partner with a business and, as soon as possible, in defining the nature and extent of the partnership. This is necessary to promote shared understanding of the partnership's goals while avoiding misunderstandings and consequent resentment. Second, a plan for open communication and resolving differences should be developed. Third, a process of evaluation should be created to keep the partnership growing and effective. Hopkins and Wendel (1997) also emphasized these strategies for successful school-business partnerships. These authors argued that without a co-created plan for partnerships, good communication, and an evaluation process, schools might feel that their authority is being usurped by businesses, and businesses may be unable to understand the inner workings of schools.

UNIVERSITY PARTNERSHIPS

Like businesses, universities are increasingly found in partnership with schools. As community partners, universities play an important and unique role. They have the potential to increase the collaborative capacity of key stakeholders through the provision of professional development. They also may bring an expertise that aids in the formal evaluation of school-community initiatives. Melaville (1998) offered additional reasons for the rise of university-school partnerships:

Universities bring a high degree of credibility and organizational capacity to the creation of school-community initiatives. What has really fueled the entry of universities into school-partnerships, however, is their discovery of untapped laboratories for service, learning, and research right in their backyards. (p. 23)

Examples and studies of university partnerships are increasingly found in the community involvement literature. These partnerships are diverse. While some universities partner with district leaders (Newbold, 1996), others partner directly with schools and other community institutions (Walsh, Andersson, & Smyer, 1999). Some university-involved initiatives focus on enhancing instruction in schools (Abell, 2000; Beyerbach, Weber, Swift, & Gooding, 1996; Richmond, 1996; Skeele & Daly, 1999); others focus on student achievement (Tucker et al., 1995), school reform (Badiali, Flora, Johnson, & Shiveley, 2000), or increasing parent involvement in schools (Bermudez & Padron, 1988). Still others focus on exposing students to career opportunities, such as those in the health sciences (Yonezawa, Thornton, & Stringfield, 1998).

The literature on effective university partnerships also emphasizes the importance of a shared vision, open communication, processes for joint decision making, and reflective evaluation. Case studies (Borthwick, 1995; Stevens, 1999), however, suggest that these key components are often difficult to establish and maintain.

An evaluation of an ongoing partnership between Dunbar High School and Johns Hopkins Medical Center serves as an illustration (Yonezawa, Thornton, & Stringfield, 1998). The partnership was developed to "expose all . . . students to information about health careers, and to ensure that students were prepared to transition from school to health careers through post-secondary education and/or post-secondary employment" (p. 2). Although the partnership was successful in increasing the number of internships for seniors, there were challenges to its implementation. Primary among these was creating an inclusive, egalitarian leadership structure that acknowledged each member's importance. This challenge was exacerbated by the reality of urban school staffing and resource shortages that slowed the initiative's progress.

Although several factors may pose challenges for particular school-university partnerships, a common challenge is the noncollaborative culture of most universities (Lawson & Hooper-Briar, 1994). Yet several studies (Benton, Zath, & Hensley, 1996; Teitel, 1994; Walsh, Andersson, & Smyer, 1999) suggest that school-university partnerships often serve as catalysts for greater collaboration within the university. When partnering with an elementary school and a local YMCA to "improve the life chances of children and families in the local community" (Walsh et al., 1999, p. 183), faculty at Boston College realized that to be most effective, they had to first unite across disciplines—education, psychology, law. They then had to work through differences with school and YMCA partners to co-create a common vision. The creation of such a vision was aided by the partners' shared beliefs about human development and students' learning. Another element important to the process of creating a common vision was that members of the initiative learned to share the role of expert, identifying and drawing on each partner's individual strengths (Walsh et al., 1999).

Universities are increasingly partnering with schools and school districts to provide professional development and training for collaboration. One example of this type of partnership is the Connections Project, sponsored by William Woods University in Missouri (Newbold, 1996). Connections was designed to help schools develop integrated service programs, build the foundation for school districts to develop partnerships with community organizations and agencies, and ensure that prospective teachers were fully prepared to collaborate with other service professionals. To meet this last goal, the university incorporated collaborative training in its teacher education program through interdisciplinary seminars for new student teachers.

Other universities are engaged in intensive collaboration with school administrators and teachers in the creation of professional development schools (PDS). Successful PDSs create innovative coalitions of universities, schools of education, and public schools that support the preparation and ongoing professional development of teachers and encourage research related to educational practice (Darling-Hammond, 1994; Levine, 1997; Sandholtz & Finan, 1998; Sirotnik & Goodlad, 1988). Creating effective PDSs requires that university faculty and administrators and school faculty and administrators engage in a collaborative process to redesign conventional teacher education practices, often in the face of organizational and attitudinal resistance (Burstein, Kretschmer, Smith, & Gudoski, 1999; Ebert, 1997; Sandholtz & Finan, 1998). Successful initiatives require individuals who are comfortable in multiple domains and can facilitate meaningful dialogue and shared decision making across interprofessional, intraprofessional, and experiential boundaries (Badiali et al., 2000). These facilitators can help PDSs to realize their potential to reform and reenergize educational institutions and processes (Burstein et al., 1999; Ebert, 1997).

SERVICE LEARNING PARTNERSHIPS

Service learning partnerships, although not as prevalent in the literature as partnerships with businesses and universities, are another popular form of community involvement in schools. Advocates of service learning argue that while education and intellectual achievement are necessary aspects of public education, equally important is a focus on community and civic participation. Ruggenberg (1993) argued that without the balance of both, "we give students the impression that acts of courage, compassion, duty, and commitment are rare, and surely done by extraordinary people; people much different from them" (p. 13).

Service learning partnerships provide students with opportunities to assist individuals or agencies in addressing social and environmental problems or community needs. Field experiences can include working with emotionally or physically disabled children, planting community gardens, or assisting with infant care in local hospitals. The goals of service learning include building stronger neighborhoods and communities, creating more active and involved citizens, and "reinvigorating traditional classrooms" (Halsted & Schine, 1994, p. 251).

Like the literature on partnerships with businesses, and universities, the literature on service learning projects also emphasizes the importance of careful, inclusive planning for program success. Such planning is needed to ensure that students have the opportunity to engage in meaningful activities. Ruggenberg (1993) contended that service learning is unproductive for students if their work is redundant or they feel that the tasks they perform are menial rather than meaningful. Students with service learning placements should be given the opportunity to actively test and utilize their strengths in positions that allow them to act instead of simply observing.

Careful planning that includes teachers, administrators, and supervisors of the field experiences also is required to successfully incorporate students' service learning projects into the school curriculum, which should be adapted to include opportunities for students to reflect on their service learning experiences and to tie them to academic content (Halsted & Schine, 1994). Students also need opportunities to analyze the consequences of their work with authority figures at school and on the job (Ruggenberg, 1993). Studies suggest that when tied to coursework, service learning helps students to gain a more comprehensive understanding of academic subjects (Alvarado, 1997) and positively affects their reflective judgment (Eyler, Lynch, & Gray, 1997). Furthermore, without attention to the "why" behind service learning projects, students may view them as another requirement to be met and forgotten (Jones & Hill, 2003).

While some initiatives (Alvarado, 1997; Ruggenberg, 1993) have successfully mobilized key stakeholders to engage in the research, design, and implementation of relevant service learning opportunities, others have found such collaboration challenging. In a case study of a service learning project at Stanford University, Service Learning Center 2000, the authors found that engaging all relevant parties in the planning process was a major obstacle to realizing the Center's goals (Hill & Pope, 1995). The Stanford project draws attention to the importance of educators and other service professionals who possess collaborative skills and can mobilize all stakeholders around a common vision. This fact, which also emerges in other forms of school-community collaboration, is arguably most evident in school-linked service integration initiatives.

SCHOOL-LINKED SERVICE INTEGRATION

School-linked service integration initiatives have increased in popularity and prevalence since the early 1990s (Behrman, 1992; Kagan, Goffin, Golub, & Pritchard, 1995). As observed by Crowson and Boyd (1993),

> Among the many strategies for strengthening school-family and school-community connections in urban education, school-centered or school linked coordination of children's services has captured much of the attention. (p. 171)

Skrtic and Sailor (1996) argued that the rising tide of interest in school-linked service integration stems from "the observations of educators and other human services professionals that if children's basic needs are not met, then these children cannot respond to even the best efforts to promote their learning through education" (p. 277).

Through school-linked service integration efforts, schools, social service agencies, and health providers attempt to provide more efficient service to children and families who need it (Dryfoos, 1994; Jehl & Kirst, 1992; Kirst & McLaughlin, 1990). Service integration initiatives can come about at different levels. They can occur among chief executive officers at local and state agencies; this level is often referred to as *service coordination*. It consists of interagency councils working to blend programmatic initiatives for the state's health and human services departments. Some state-led initiatives encourage the parallel formation of local interagency councils to extend service coordination from state to locality, while other initiatives encourage local service coordination with no parallel development among state agencies themselves (Crowson & Boyd, 1993). However, it is generally agreed that coordination and support at the state level is necessary if initiatives at the local level are to be sustained over time (Burch & Palanki, 1995; Epstein, 1991; Stone, 1995; Sullivan & Sugarman, 1996).

A second level at which service integration initiatives can occur is among frontline service providers from different agencies who work together to provide clients with a coordinated service plan. At this level, professionals share knowledge, responsibility, and support (Stone, 1995). Service integration also can occur between on-site service providers and the parents and families they serve (Bruner, 1991; Burch & Palanki, 1995; Stone, 1995). At this level, empowerment and voice are extended to parents and other family members as the beneficiaries, consumers, or end users of the services provided.

Documented benefits of school-linked service integration initiatives include behavioral and academic gains for students who receive intensive services, such as those involved in California's Healthy Start programs (Newman, 1995). Research also has shown improved student attendance, immunization rates, and student conduct at schools providing coordinated services, such as Freedom Elementary School in California (Amato, 1996) and Quitman Street Community School in New Jersey (Dryfoos, 2003). Increased parent involvement in schools also has been a documented outcome of some coordinated service programs (Burch & Palanki, 1995; Dryfoos, 2003; Stallings, 1995). Studies further suggest that through integrated service programs, more students and families who need intensive services receive them (Amato, 1996). Contrary to popular belief, however, there is no evidence that such initiatives are more cost-effective than traditional methods of service provision. "Indeed," as observed by Crowson and Boyd (1993), "the costs of management, in effective children's service coordination, can increase" (p. 160). Dryfoos (2003) suggests that a full-service community school open all year costs approximately $1,000 per student per year in addition to the cost of traditional schooling.

Beyond documenting benefits, the literature documents key challenges to the effective development and implementation of service integration initiatives (Crowson & Boyd, 1993; Dolan, 1992; Jehl & Kirst, 1992; Sullivan & Sugarman, 1996; Wynn, Costello, Halpern, & Richman, 1994; Wynn, Merry, & Berg, 1995). The challenges faced by such programs are similar to those previously discussed and largely center on developing structures and processes that engender and support collaboration among key stakeholders.

Interagency and interprofessional rivalries over issues of turf and "knowing" are major obstacles to successful service integration initiatives. Rivalries generally develop among collaborators due to a lack of knowledge about the methods and procedures of other service agencies, a lack of understanding about the role of other service providers, and an undervaluing of other service providers' contributions. Differences in professional certification standards, accounting and auditing procedures, funding streams, confidentiality requirements, and eligibility restrictions all can create obstacles to interagency collaboration (Sullivan & Sugarman, 1996).

Some suggest that training service providers for collaboration is one way to address the rivalries and misunderstandings that appear to be a ubiquitous feature of service coordination programs (Burch & Palanki, 1995; Stone, 1995). Such training would help professionals involved in school-linked service integration initiatives to acquire the skills and interprofessional information sharing and language systems they need to be effective. Based on their work with professional educators in Utah, Gallagher, Knowlton, Mahlios, and Kleinhammer-Tramill (1997) argued that in order to achieve a reasonable level of collaboration among service providers, "we must find ways to address and counter the conditions that define the nature and quality of teachers' daily work and thus their ability to collaborate with other professionals" (p. 15). The authors observed that the professional development of teachers and many other service professionals lacks any significant element of collaboration or interprofessional exchange.

Given this reality, a neutral party of some sort is generally needed to coordinate service integration programs if they are to be successful (Dryfoos, 1998, 2003; Gray, 1991; Molloy et al., 1995). A neutral party would ensure that processes were developed to promote communication, understanding, and participation across professional agencies and with families and communities.

Lack of family and community participation in the planning and development of many school-linked service coordination programs is another issue that can reduce the effectiveness of these initiatives (Burch & Palanki, 1995; Stone, 1995). Families often have little meaningful involvement in the planning, implementation, or direction of school-linked service coordination programs (Keith, 1996). Furthermore, many such initiatives do not change the fundamental structures of school management so that schools are more accessible to families and communities (Cohen, 1991). Indeed, Skrtic and Sailor (1996) argued that without attention to the principles of voice, participation, and inclusion, efforts to integrate educational, social welfare, and public health services and to link them to local communities will not realize their potential to transform relations between schools and communities.

FAITH-BASED PARTNERSHIPS

Faith-based organizations are defined as self-identified religious groups or institutions from a wide variety of traditions that include but are not limited to various Christian, Jewish, Islamic, Buddhist, and Hindu groups. This definition is not meant to ignore the existence or importance of other faith-based organizations but simply to narrow the focus on a very broad topic.

The relationship between U.S. public schools and faith-based organizations has not been without conflict. Both groups have engaged in heated legal and philosophical battles over issues such as school prayer and other forms of religious expression, school vouchers, the place of creationism in the teaching of science, government funding, and the role of religious values in public schooling.

In contrast to such conflict and divisiveness, there has been an equally prominent movement toward collaboration, coordination, and cooperation. The spirit of this movement is reflected in a guide jointly published by the American Jewish Congress, the Christian Legal Society, and the First Amendment Center at Vanderbilt University (1999) and endorsed by national educational and faith-based groups. The introduction to the guide states,

> By working together in ways that are permissible under the First Amendment, as interpreted by the U.S. Supreme Court, schools and religious communities can do much to enhance the mission of public education. (p. 1)

Although constitutionally prohibited from proselytizing, recruiting, or imposing religious views and doctrines on students, faith-based organizations can participate in public school reform in a variety of ways, as illustrated by the following examples (unless otherwise indicated, the examples are taken from Partnership for Family Involvement in Education [1999]).

Alexandria, Virginia: The faith-based community and public elementary schools in Alexandria work together to tutor children in reading. A congregation-based coordinator recruits volunteer tutors and assists with scheduling; a school-based coordinator acts as the point of contact. Classroom teachers identify children who need tutoring and assist coordinators with scheduling. Tutoring materials and training for tutors is provided by the public schools. Tutors and students meet for three thirty-minute sessions per week.

Chicago, Illinois: The Chicago Public Schools Interfaith Community Partnership, a multicultural group of religious leaders, assists local schools in addressing issues such as student discipline, truancy and low attendance rates, school safety, and student and staff attitudes and interactions. The partnership provides crisis intervention services and workshops for parents, undertakes curriculum development in the area of character and values, and sponsors radio and television interviews with public school staff to promote Chicago public school initiatives.

Washington, D.C.: Shiloh Baptist Church in Washington, D.C., established a learning center to teach critical thinking and problem-solving skills to children in Grades 4–8 by using a math-, science-, and computer-based curriculum. The center, which is staffed by both paid employees and volunteers, is open after school and during the evening. During the daytime, the center is used to teach adults job skills in a welfare-to-work program. The church also has established a reading tutorial program for children attending Seaton

Elementary School and a program called the Male and Female Youth Enhancement Project. The project is designed to encourage healthy lifestyles in African American youth between the ages of eight and fifteen by providing them with positive role models and educational and social activities.

The effectiveness of such programs rests largely on the quality of implementation. However, when well planned and executed, these partnerships have been found to be beneficial for targeted students. For example, Gardner et al. (2001) found that an afterschool program implemented through a partnership between a local church, a public school, and Ohio State University's College of Education had significant effects on the reading and mathematics achievement of the ten male students who participated in the program. The students were enrolled in Grades 3–5, were at least one year below grade level (as measured by Ohio's state proficiency tests), and were experiencing social-behavioral problems before entering the program. Eight males from the church and five preservice teachers volunteered for the program. They were trained by university faculty to provide social and academic support to participants using peer-mediated strategies. The program was housed at the church, was offered five days per week, and began directly after school, at 3:30 p.m.

Analysis of pretest and posttest results showed that all students improved their reading scores on the Slosson Oral Reading Test and their accuracy and fluency rates on multiplication facts—both targeted academic skills. Gardner et al. (2001) concluded,

> The Mount Olivet afterschool program provides a unique opportunity for all invested members (i.e., urban schools, parents, at-risk students, university teacher preparation programs, community resources) to be involved in a positive solution that addresses the problems of poor test scores among urban students. (pp. 9–10)

Before entering into partnerships, however, educators and leaders of faith-based organizations should understand and abide by the following principles:

- Public schools must be neutral concerning religion in all of their activities.
- Students have the right to engage in religious activities as long as they do not interfere with the rights of others, and they have the right not to engage in those activities.
- Participation in programs is not limited to religious groups.
- A student's grades, class ranking, or participation in any school program is not affected by his or her decision to participate or not participate in a cooperative program with a religious institution.

- Student participation in any cooperative program is not conditioned on membership in any religious group, acceptance or rejection of any religious belief, or participation (or refusal to participate) in any religious activity.

(For more information see American
Jewish Congress, Christian Legal Society, and the
First Amendment Center, Vanderbilt University, 1999.)

Mutual understanding and acceptance of these principles help to ensure that all stakeholders' rights are protected, especially those of the students for whom school-community partnerships are primarily designed.

SUMMARY

This chapter highlights three factors that influence the effectiveness of schools' collaboration with diverse community partnerships: a shared vision, clearly defined roles and responsibilities, and open communication.

Shared Vision

In order for successful partnerships to develop, participants must have a common vision. When such a shared vision exists, partnerships are more likely to develop in a manner that is satisfactory to all parties and to meet their stated goals. With more complex partnerships, building consensus on scope, direction, and goals can require tremendous effort. Dryfoos (2003) describes the collaborative process in the following way:

It should be acknowledged at the outset that collaboration is hard work: it takes endless time, meetings, patience, and understanding. Schools and community agencies have to learn each other's language, mores, concepts, and prejudices. (p. 205)

To achieve the desired benefits for students' learning, schools and community partners cannot bypass this important aspect of partnering.

Clearly Defined Roles and Responsibilities

The literature on school-community partnerships also emphasizes the importance of clearly defined roles and responsibilities. All partners should understand what they are expected to contribute. Without clearly defined expectations, misunderstandings can ensue that jeopardize the partnership's effectiveness. For example, in any community partnership in which privately owned facilities are used, it is critical to clarify the roles and responsibilities of individual parties regarding the preparation, use, maintenance, and supervision of the facilities.

Open Communication

Open communication—the process through which shared visions are created and roles and responsibilities are articulated—is the foundation for any successful partnership. It also is critical to carrying out other collaborative processes, including shared decision making, conflict management, and reflection and evaluation.

These factors prominently highlight the need for reflection and preparation before collaborations begin. School leaders can begin this process by considering the following five questions. Answers to these questions will help schools to assess their levels of readiness for collaboration and the levels of partnership complexity for which they are prepared.

1. *What is your school's vision of excellence?* What is it that you want your school known for? There is an old adage, "If you don't know where you are going, you probably won't get there." School leaders, with faculty members, parents, and community partners, should construct a commonly shared vision of excellence for their school before planning community partnerships.

2. *What is the goal that this partnership will help to achieve?* Community partnerships should be developed to achieve important school goals. Whether school-, student-, family-, or community-focused, school-community partnerships should be implemented to move a school closer to a vision of excellence. Many schools may be tempted to enter a partnership without clear purpose, solely to meet external requirements, expectations, or guidelines. Despite such pressures, school leaders should maintain a measured, purposeful approach to community partnership development. Furthermore, in order to measure the success of a partnership, it is important to have not only a clear goal but also some measurable indicators of success.

3. *What school resources, including time, space, and personnel, will the partnership require?* School-community partnerships, whether simple or complex, require some effort, from writing and mailing a letter of thanks to training community volunteers. Before entering a partnership, a school should realistically assess its capacity to exert the needed effort. Such an assessment will help school leaders to decide on the appropriateness of an alliance or perhaps determine needed modifications. Furthermore, school leaders should communicate

openly with potential community partners to ensure that they too understand and can commit to the required resource exchange.

4. *Is the community partnership project in compliance with school, district, and state guidelines?* No two states, districts, or schools are exactly alike. Some districts have very strict rules regarding school-community partnerships and the types and value of resources being exchanged. Other districts have few or no restrictions, leaving the final say with school principals. Likewise, some districts encourage individual schools, and some schools encourage individual teachers to engage in community partnerships. Others require that a central authority arrange such partnerships. Before beginning community partnerships, then, schools should take the time to investigate building and district policies to avoid later misunderstandings.

5. *Who in the school will be responsible for overseeing partnership planning, implementation, and evaluation?* As suggested in the previous chapter and as will be further explored in Chapter 3, a team approach helps schools to successfully plan and implement schoolwide partnerships without overtaxing one individual. School leadership or site-based management teams, for example, can be organized into committees, one of which could be responsible for working with others in the school and local community to incorporate family and community involvement in school improvement plans and activities. Several variations of this approach are encouraged and indeed required by the National Network of Partnership Schools (see Epstein et al., 2002).

   A team or committee focused on partnerships should assign members to planning, implementation, and evaluation tasks that are required for partnership program development, such as developing and monitoring budgets, maintaining records, and corresponding with partners. The team leader, therefore, must be amenable to distributed or shared leadership. A successful team leader might be an assistant principal, an experienced teacher, or a home-school coordinator with well-honed collaborative skills. It is also important that the team leader is committed to the role and has the time necessary to honor the commitment. Because time is so critical, on many teams, leadership responsibilities are shared in a co-chair arrangement.

School-community partnerships, then, especially as they increase in complexity, require forethought and planning on the part of educational leaders. Schools must achieve a certain level of readiness in order for such partnerships to thrive. Schools that have achieved this level of readiness have key components in place. These components are described in Chapter 3.

3 Components of Successful Community Partnerships

C ase study and survey research of NNPS elementary, middle, and high schools[6] suggest that several components may determine whether schools succeed or fail to develop comprehensive community partnerships that range in complexity and that achieve important goals for students' success. The interrelated components are (a) a high-functioning school, (b) a student-centered environment, (c) an effective partnership team, (d) principal leadership, and (e) external support. When in place, these components help schools attract a variety of suitable partners and address common challenges to effective partnership program development.

HIGH-FUNCTIONING SCHOOLS

Research suggests that NNPS schools that effectively developed and maintained comprehensive community partnerships over time were high-functioning institutions, which made them attractive to potential community partners. These schools were goal oriented and well organized, with committees that were focused on defined areas for school improvement. For example, Patty Simmons,[7] a faculty member at the suburban case high school, noted,

> It is a very organized institution and that is one thing that I really like. People know where they are headed; there is a plan in place for just

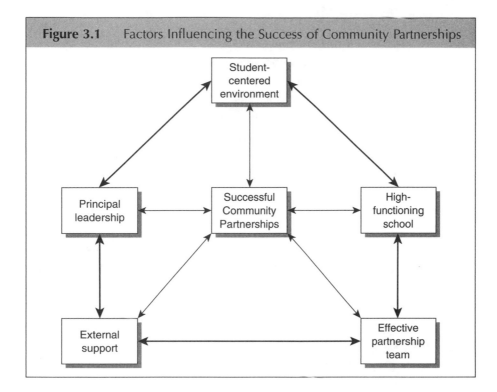

Figure 3.1 Factors Influencing the Success of Community Partnerships

about everything if not everything in this school. They are very clear about their goals and their purposes and what is expected of you, which I think is very important. They have high expectations not only for their students but for us as educators, which I think is a good thing.

The case schools also were highly regarded in their communities, districts, and states. They were known for their academic and athletic achievements and progress, as well as their community outreach. All case schools had received district, state, or national awards, which further enhanced their reputations. Yet far from resting on their laurels, these schools actively sought avenues for continued improvement. Greg Fig, the suburban high school principal, observed,

We are in the top 1% of all schools in the state . . . right now in terms of academic achievement. I think it is that pressure, maybe pressure isn't the right word, but it is the emphasis that the parents place on the value of education that really keeps everyone on their toes.

Similarly, when describing how she determined whether to partner with a community-based organization, an elementary school principal explained,

"If I think that is something that is going to be a positive good for children, then basically that's how I determine if the school will pursue it."

Because of their focus on improvement, the schools regularly evaluated their goals, encouraging input from all stakeholders—parents, students, teachers, and community members. It is interesting that while many schools endure high turnover, the case schools were able to maintain their administrators, faculty, and staff, which contributed to their high levels of functioning.

When transitions did occur, these high-functioning schools worked to make them as smooth as possible. For example, during the course of our research, two of the case schools experienced changes in principals. In each case, however, the assistant principal took on the role after months of working with the retiring principal to ensure that the schools' goals, values, and basic programs were maintained. Thus amid change, these schools were able to maintain high levels of continuity, which further contributed to the quality of their schools' programs.

STUDENT-CENTERED LEARNING ENVIRONMENTS

NNPS case schools that achieved success with community partnerships also placed students' academic achievement and personal success at the center of the improvement efforts. Community partnerships were seen as part of the schools' overall strategy to support students and not as something "additional" to do.

The case schools were adamant about their support of students. In the following excerpt, Kathy Drum, the principal at the urban high school, explained her expectations of faculty and staff:

> You came into this profession not for the money I know, not because you thought it was going to be an easy job, you couldn't have possibly thought that. If you did, you found out that you were wrong! So if you are here for the good of kids, then you do what is best and what is right for kids. That is my whole take on anything, not just the proficiency test but across the board. We have got to do things that are going to be right and the best that we know how to do for our kids. I don't want a kid to leave here not feeling as though they have really been prepared for out there, because it is not easy out there with no education. So I just keep preaching and preaching, to not only my staff but to the students as well, that you have got to take this seriously; this is our future.

Similarly, Deborah Foster, the principal at the elementary school, stated,

> My primary goal as school leader is to make sure that our students achieve. . . . I must make sure that instruction takes place on a daily basis in every classroom and that every child is exposed to the best that we have to give them as far as the curriculum. That is my first and primary goal—achievement.

The case schools also wanted their students to be well-rounded individuals who understood their responsibilities to themselves and others. The rural high school, for example, focused on students giving to one another and to their communities through volunteer work. The suburban and urban high schools established extensive internship programs to expose their students to different careers, individuals, and future possibilities. According to the urban high school principal, these internships help "mold young minds and futures, and help them to know that they can be whatever it is they dream of being."

Community partners valued the way that case schools valued students. For example, a community partner at a health care agency noted that the agency's commitment to continued collaboration with the elementary school stemmed from the school's goals for students' learning and also its nurturing attitude toward students. According to a volunteer,

> When you enter the school, the teachers are not yelling. I guess they know that the kids go through so much to get there in the morning that they don't want to push them anymore. They are there for the students.

EFFECTIVE PARTNERSHIP TEAMS

NNPS case schools with effective community connections also had effective partnership teams. NNPS requires that all school members create or identify action teams for partnerships, which should include a school administrator, teacher representatives, parent and community representatives, and other interested stakeholders who are responsible for planning and implementing school, family, and community partnership activities to achieve important school goals.[8] This team approach has several advantages over having a single individual responsible for implementing a schoolwide partnership program.

First, a team approach allows for multiple and diverse voices to be involved in all stages of partnership program development, from the selection of goals and foci to the evaluation of practices. Parents and community members can offer perspectives to educators that add to their understanding of the students with whom they work. These insights, coupled with educators' professional insights and knowledge, can help all parties develop a more holistic view of the needs and talents of students. This approach not only increases the likelihood of shared ownership, which is vitally important for partnership program success, it also helps to challenge stereotypical views and perceptions that can hinder collaborative efforts to improve student learning.

Furthermore, because the work of building a partnership program is shared, a team approach reduces the responsibilities of each individual member and consequently the likelihood of individual burnout. Finally, because a team structure can remain constant even as members change, a team approach increases the likelihood that partnerships will become a permanent part of schools' overall improvement program.

The case schools' Action Teams for Partnerships (ATPs) were well-functioning teams led by seasoned educators. Some ATP leaders were experienced teachers and others were building administrators. Novices or those new to the profession were members of the teams but were not team leaders. ATP leaders, while understanding the importance of their role, emphasized the need for a team structure for partnership program development. Drew Collier, Urban High's ATP chairperson, stated,

> I think that you have to understand, number one, that you can't do it all yourself, that you do need the help of other people. And then you also have to understand that people need a leader, they need to see someone take that primary role. . . . The leadership should be interchangeable. Nothing should just fall apart because something happens to that person who is in charge. That is what you ultimately want to accomplish.

The membership of these teams was diverse, and each member had a clear role to play. For example, some had close links to the community and facilitated community outreach, some had technological expertise needed for Web site development, and some had expertise in evaluation strategies. The following interview excerpts from Patty Simmons and Cassandra Bridges, the ATP members at the suburban and urban case high schools, respectively, serve as illustration:

> When I joined, they were trying to divvy up the committees, and one of their goals last year was to get a Web site going. Since I have the training, I volunteered to do that for us.

Because of my ties with the community, with the business sector and with these various agencies that we need in order to get the kids hired, Ms. Benjamin looked at me as a possibility for being on the partnership committee.

Because of their reputations for effectiveness, which developed over time, the ATPs did not have difficulty attracting and keeping active members. Members generally volunteered and expressed a genuine commitment to the school-community partnerships. When asked about the source of this commitment, Pete Collier, an ATP member at the urban high school who is also the school's PTA president, offered the following explanation:

The best word I can think of is *love* because they are people who are putting something in and the only thing that they are getting out is gratification of seeing someone else being successful in life.

The teams met regularly, usually once per month as evidenced by the agendas and minutes examined, and systematically planned community partnership activities to achieve schoolwide improvement goals. While some partnership teams primarily focused on increasing parent and community participation, others were more focused on student achievement and attendance goals.

Research conducted at urban elementary, middle, and high schools that have been less successful in developing school-community partnerships shows the importance of effective teams. At less effective schools, teams have difficulty recruiting and maintaining members, meet irregularly and do not have specific roles and tasks, are led by teachers who have little or no experience in collaborative leadership, or some combination of these factors (Sanders & Epstein, 2000).

ATP effectiveness supported the case schools' capacity to build successful community partnerships. These teams acknowledged challenges, especially during the initial years when they grappled with identity and goal formation; however, they faced those obstacles, learned from those experiences, and evolved into the central engines of the schools' partnership programs.

PRINCIPAL LEADERSHIP

The school effectiveness literature emphasizes the importance of strong principal leadership for high-functioning schools. Principal leadership has been linked either directly or indirectly to a number of favorable school outcomes.

These include high student achievement, teacher commitment and efficacy, and family and community involvement and participation (Hallinger & Heck, 1996; Rinehart, Short, & Short, 1998). Principals who model for faculty and staff a genuine openness to parent and community involvement; establish an expectation for dialogue and communication among school personnel, families, communities, and students; and support others in developing leadership in the area of family and community involvement create school cultures that are ripe for collaboration (Carr, 1997; Sanders & Harvey, 2002).

Each of the case high schools had principals who exhibited these leadership qualities. These principals were not always members of the partnership teams, yet they identified school personnel to lead these teams who had the skills, expertise, and experience to be successful. Furthermore, the principals were fully aware and supportive of the teams' efforts, providing needed resources, attending community partnership events, arranging class coverage for teachers attending ATP meetings, and acknowledging and praising partnership efforts and successes. In so doing, they facilitated community partnership development.

The principals in the case schools identified with the notion of being facilitative leaders. Dr. Greg Fig, Albert Harrison, and Kathy Drum, principals at the suburban, rural, and urban case high schools, respectively, offered the following comments:

> I think that my role has been more of a facilitator than it has been anything else. I also think that my job is to make sure that the staff in this school remains focused on our objectives. It is very easy.

> I try to make things happen as the facilitator of things that the teachers want to see happen, that the students want to see happen, that parents want to see happen. You are very much involved in that facilitating role. You are also a great many different things to a great many different people, and your role changes.

> I am a facilitator. They will of course share the information with me, but I don't block anything that they are trying to do as long as it makes sense. I want them to generate more community-parent involvement. I want them to know that they have my support with what they are doing.

Some principals, like Albert Harrison, not only served as internal facilitators but helped their action team connect to groups outside of the school:

My role is to connect the people in the school with the people out of the school, to be a contact person in terms of putting these groups together. . . . So that is the role of the principal, I think, to connect the groups so that they fulfill each other's partnership relationship.

In their roles as facilitators and partners in school improvement, these principals were not threatened by the fact that other administrators, action team leaders, parents, or students had creative solutions to school challenges. Kathy Drum, principal at the urban high school, for example, described her leadership style in the following way:

I'm not one to say, Well this won't work, that won't work. If you have something and it sounds reasonable, then fine. Until we find out that it won't work, then let's try it because you don't know. It is obvious that what we have been doing hasn't worked, so why should I be closed to a new idea? It doesn't matter whether it is my idea or not; I don't care. If you have something that is going to work then . . . let's do it.

Although the case schools had successful community partnerships, they still lacked different types of resources, such as space and funding that would have further enhanced their programs. When possible, principals showed their support by finding innovative ways to meet such needs. For example, at the urban high school, the principal identified space for a parent and community center. In the following passage, Urban High's ATP chair, Drew Collier, described the importance of this gesture:

That meeting room is a big deal because I can't think of any other high school that has a designated area for parents and the community to meet. That was a real commitment on her behalf, especially because . . . we have teachers that are floating [who do not have permanent classrooms]. That's a big deal, and it really shows that the administration is in favor of what we are doing.

The importance of principal leadership for successful school-community partnerships cannot be overstated. Indeed, a qualitative study of teacher leadership for community involvement in three urban middle schools (Sanders, in press) found that lack of active principal support was a primary obstacle to successful community outreach. None of the principals withheld permission for the teachers to pursue the projects, and each acknowledged at some point during the course of the projects that they would be valuable for students and the school. However, teachers leading the projects wanted their principals to help disseminate information about the community-based projects, help to mobilize and coordinate building support for the projects, and, minimally, recognize and support their efforts.

The frustration these teachers felt when such support was not forthcoming is illustrated in the following journal excerpts written by Monica and Jessica, two teachers employed at one of the middle schools involved in the study:

> **Monica—October 30:** Today the principal sent home a letter to all students' families. The focus of the letter was twofold. The first was to explain the importance of reading at home, and the second was to explain programs at our school to increase student achievement. . . . He was informed of the book project Jessica and I were starting, yet he did not even mention it in his letter.

> **Jessica—November 14:** We also spoke to the principal today, just to make sure he knew what was going on. . . . He didn't say a word of thanks, not even a positive comment. It's so typical, and that's why he will lose Monica and me in the next couple of years. A word or two of appreciation or encouragement can mean everything.

Without active principal support, the teachers felt unsupported and unappreciated, and they reacted accordingly. Their momentum and willingness to extend themselves beyond their formal job descriptions diminished over the course of the study. Not surprisingly, the community involvement projects were not continued into the following school year.

EXTERNAL SUPPORT

Finally, the NNPS schools that attracted and maintained community partnerships over time also had and took full advantage of external support from state and district offices of parent and community involvement. According to McLaughlin (1992), districts have a facilitative role to play in building schools' individual and organizational capacity for reform. She argued that through the provision of direct support; the facilitation of ongoing dialogue and feedback about educational practice; and the celebration of professional commitment, engagement, and progress, district leaders can significantly influence the quality with which school reforms are implemented. Similarly, Mitchell and Raphael (1999) found that state departments of education, through policy creation, direction, and guidance, influenced school and district implementation of reform strategies.

States

The case schools received various types of assistance from their states. Some states provided training opportunities while others provided funding, either directly in the form of incentive grants or through district partnership programs. The urban high school, for example, was a recipient of several annual state grants for partnerships. When discussing the importance of such grants, Principal Kathy Drum stated,

> It was a plus to get these grants. It gives you the opportunity to do what you may not have funding to do otherwise. It gives you that little cushion. You can say, "Wait a minute, now we can do this."

Districts

The case schools also were in districts that supported them in numerous ways. These districts offered planning assistance, training, and administrative support. Molly Shaw, a district facilitator for the suburban high school, described her role in the following way:

> I am the districtwide volunteer coordinator. . . . There are no set hours. When they need help, they call. I meet once a month with the volunteer coordinators at each school for about an hour. I meet with principals and attend PTA, PTO, and partnership meetings. I try to get to all of them to see how they are doing. If there are any problems, I try to deal with whoever is responsible for the partnership activities.

Molly worked part-time for the school district. Previously, she had been involved with the parent group at the suburban case high school and decided to take her experience to the district level.

At one point, the rural case high school also had a district facilitator, Cheryl Finn. But because of budget cuts, she became a principal at an elementary school. However, she still assisted the district and the rural high school's ATP. She contended,

> The biggest, the most important thing to community partnerships, I think, is the buy-in of administration. If the superintendent and school board members buy into a program, it makes it so much easier for you.

The rural case high school also enjoyed strong support from its district superintendent. He attended the school's action team meetings, and when he could not, he sent the assistant superintendent. Although its budget had made it impossible for the district to maintain her position, the commitment the facilitator saw from administrators and the results she saw from her work encouraged her to continue her involvement with community partnerships. Districts also supported schools' efforts to increase and maintain community partnerships through targeted training of schools' partnership teams.

SUMMARY

This chapter introduces and discusses five components of successful school-community partnerships: (a) a high-functioning school, (b) a student-centered environment, (c) an effective partnership team, (e) principal leadership, and (f) external support. These components helped NNPS schools to develop a variety of effective and meaningful community partnerships over time and to enhance their educational programs and reputations for excellence. When schools take the time to build these essential components, they increase the likelihood that their community partnerships will achieve important goals for students, as well as their families and communities.

Schools that do not have these components in place may want to limit community outreach to only simple partnership activities, as discussed in Chapter 1, while they address organizational or leadership challenges or both that their schools face. Until schools have prepared a strong foundation, seeking to develop more comprehensive and complex partnerships is akin to building a house on sand. Reputations for excellence are built one success at a time. Likewise, reputations for dysfunction are built one failure at a time. Taking the time to create an environment in which more complex community partnerships can thrive will help schools to avoid the failed projects that further limit their ability to attract and maintain desirable community partners.

In the following chapter, I describe a teacher leader's experience in opening her school's doors to community partnerships through a school literacy project. The description highlights four steps that schools can take to systematically build the components for successful community partnerships presented in this chapter.

4 Building Capacity for Successful Community Partnerships

A Vignette

To recap, to design and implement a variety of community partnerships that help to achieve a vision of excellence, schools need the components of success: (a) a high-functioning school, (b) a student-centered environment, (c) an effective partnership team, (d) principal leadership, and (e) external support, as described in Chapter 3. Schools that have yet to achieve these components, however, can still incorporate simple community partnerships in their school improvement efforts. Indeed, by doing so, schools at various stages of readiness can build their capacity for more comprehensive and complex partnerships. In this chapter, I describe how one teacher-leader moved her school closer to this goal by implementing a literacy project involving four community partners.

THE SCHOOL

The K–5 elementary school has approximately 500 students, mostly African American. Of these students, 84% is eligible for free and reduced-price meals. The school's daily attendance rate for the 2003–2004 school year was 94%, the highest it had been in over five years. Student mobility was high, with approximately 20% of students entering the school and 14% withdrawing from it during the school year. Of the student population, 20% received special education services.

THE GOAL

The elementary school is located in the center of a once bustling, but now economically struggling, area of a large industrial city. Compared to other schools in the city, it is neither highly dysfunctional nor highly functional. It is an average school that has made moderate but steady gains in students' test scores since the state established a curriculum-driven assessment system. Aside from its focus on student achievement as evidenced by gains on state and national standardized exams, when the 2004–2005 school year began, the school did not have in place any of the components described in Chapter 3.

What it did have, however, was one teacher-leader, Janet,[9] who firmly believed that school, family, and community partnerships were essential to educational excellence. Because of her background in reading and her success in the classroom, during her third year as a first-grade teacher at the school, the principal approached Janet about leading a schoolwide literacy project to increase students' reading outside of school and ultimately their performance on the state reading assessment.

THE TEAM

Janet decided that in order to make the literacy project a success, she needed to work with a team of individuals who would provide diverse perspectives and share the responsibilities as well as the potential successes and failures of the project. She was able to recruit three members, including a parent volunteer with whom she had worked closely during the year, a teacher who also was a close friend and colleague, and the school librarian who was very interested in and knowledgeable about literacy development in children. The school principal served as an ex officio member. She initially took a skeptical, hands-off approach toward the project. Although she had asked Janet to lead the project, she offered little in the way of resources, advice, or encouragement.

However, the principal's attitude did not dissuade the team from meeting bimonthly to plan, implement, and evaluate the project. Over the course of planning and implementation, the team, bound by professional interests and personal ties, worked well together. Communication was open and productive. With Janet at the helm, members were delegated a variety of tasks and held accountable by the team. As the team's experience grew, so did its effectiveness.

THE PROJECT

Because of the team's shared interest in school, family, and community partnerships, it decided to develop a literacy project that involved not only teachers and students but families and the community as well. The project had two components: One focused on increasing students' reading outside of school through a schoolwide competition. Reading logs were sent home, and families were asked to document the number of books or book chapters read to and by their children during nonschool hours. Selected fifth-grade students collected the logs each week for Janet who would chart the progress of each class on a large bulletin board in the front lobby of the school building. The class showing the greatest progress at the end of each month earned parent-organized pizza parties.

In addition to the class reading competition, the team organized monthly family literacy workshops, which focused on topics such as learning styles, motivation, vocabulary, and comprehension. Parents were encouraged to attend these workshops to learn more about supporting their children's literacy development at home. Best practice in the field suggests that parent attendance at such workshops increases when hands-on activities are included; when students perform; and when food and incentives, such as door prizes, are provided (Epstein et al., 2002; Floyd, 1998). With limited funds, the team needed support to design and implement workshops that met these standards. They turned to the community for assistance.

THE COMMUNITY PARTNERS

The school did not have a tradition of community partnerships. When the team requested a list of community partners, the principal failed to provide one. She neither supported nor objected to team members seeking the involvement of new community partners, however.

Prior to the first workshop, held in October, team members visited several local businesses, including a local grocery store chain, a nearby mall, and a florist. At each turn, they were told that the businesses could not support the school's efforts at the time. Instead of giving up, Janet and other team members continued to knock on doors.

Prior to the second workshop, held in November, the tide changed. At the suggestion of a friend who was driving in the area, Janet stopped at a local beauty salon a few blocks away from the school. The salon owner was a former student and was eager to hear about the project and support the effort. She donated gift certificates to be raffled off at the workshops and requested the opportunity to become more deeply involved in the school's improvement efforts. In turn, Janet offered to distribute flyers advertising her services at the workshops.

Another member of the team talked to the manager of a local Kentucky Fried Chicken restaurant. After listening to a description of the project, the manager agreed to provide food and beverages for the second workshop. On seeing the turnout (forty-five parent members, up from twenty-five at the first workshop) and the quality of the project, the manager agreed to provide food and beverages for each monthly workshop. Another team member contacted the manager at a local fitness center that she attended. After hearing about the project, the manager also agreed to provide free two-week membership certificates as door prizes and volunteered to speak briefly to parents about family health and physical activity at the third workshop. Janet and another team member also visited a local community-based organization that distributes free, gently used books to organizations throughout the city. The teachers selected dozens of books to give away as incentives and rewards during the workshops.

THE RESULTS

Faculty, students, parents, and, of special importance, the principal, viewed the literacy project as a major success. Indeed, after the second workshop with its notable increase in parent attendance, the principal donated dessert for the monthly events and invited central office personnel to witness the success of the project. While student test results were not yet in, reading logs indicated that students and their families read a great deal during nonschool hours, and students were recognized for their efforts. The logs also provide the school with useful data. Younger children reported more family reading and exchange than older students at the school. Promoting family literacy practices with older students is an area on which the school could concentrate more attention and resources.

Also, parent participation in the workshops was well beyond expectations. While attendance at monthly PTO meetings averaged four parents, attendance at the literacy workshops averaged thirty-five parents and was as high as fifty parents. It is unclear whether this was the result of community involvement; however, the resources and support offered by community partners helped the school to provide workshops that met best practice standards for family involvement activities.

Over the course of the monthly workshops, dozens of family members learned more about how to support their children's literacy development. Because different grade levels performed at the beginning of each workshop (with songs, readings, presentations, etc.), a broad spectrum of parents was reached. For those who did not attend, the team summarized the information provided during the workshops in the school's monthly newsletters. The school's community partners were informed of these results and thanked for their participation and support.

LESSONS LEARNED

As a result of Janet's leadership, her school is closer to achieving the components described in Chapter 3. Her principal is now more supportive of and open to community partnerships, and her school has the nucleus of an effective partnership team. This project, thus, highlights four steps that other schools can take to build their capacity for more comprehensive community partnerships: (a) start with a school priority, (b) work collaboratively, (c) be persistent when seeking community partners, and (d) communicate regularly and widely.

Start With a School Priority

Most schools have one or more goals that they wish to achieve. This is especially true in the current school reform environment that emphasizes statewide standards and accountability. School goals may include improved attendance, improved student performance on state or other standardized assessments, increased parent involvement, or other quality measures. When community partnerships are included in strategies that target such goals, they receive greater principal support and underscore the importance and utility of community involvement in schools' improvement efforts.

As Janet's story illustrates, community partnerships should be part of a well-planned strategy to achieve a specific goal. A well-planned project, based on best practice in the field, is likely to be successful, and will have legitimacy in the eyes of the school principal and the community partners. When teachers, parents, and other school leaders approach community partnerships in this manner, they help their school to build its capacity for more comprehensive and complex partnerships in the future.

Work Collaboratively

While Janet had a professional background in reading and a keen interest in family and community involvement, she could not have planned, implemented, and evaluated the literacy project alone. Building on the personal and professional relationships she had developed during her tenure at the school, she assembled a team that provided the support, expertise, and energy needed to carry out the literacy project. Through teamwork, more community partners were identified, tasks were shared, and plans were developed and refined through group synergy.

A team, however, is as effective as its leader. Janet was responsible for keeping the team focused on its goals, keeping momentum and energy for the project high, ensuring that team members had manageable tasks and responsibilities as well as the resources and support necessary to carry them out, and creating a climate of cooperation and encouragement. These are the responsibilities and opportunities of collaborative leadership. For those school leaders who would like to learn about or review the basics of collaborative leadership, Hank Rubin's (2002), *Collaborative Leadership* offers a useful overview.

Be Persistent

As Janet's story illustrates, when it comes to finding community partners, persistence is important. Because her school did not have an established history of community partnerships and the principal did not share the list of community partners that were connected to the school, Janet and the project team were required to identify new community partners. Initially, it appeared that no community partner wanted to participate. Indeed, for the first workshop, Janet purchased a gift certificate to raffle because no community group had responded to the team's request. If Janet and the team had not been persistent, the four community partners who eventually became involved would not have been approached. Persistence counts.

Not everyone is comfortable asking potential community partners for help. Let those who are more comfortable take the lead. As a team, brainstorm the key points that should be addressed when approaching a community partner. Also, follow up oral requests with written communication. This communication is important to thank the partner for participation, confirm what was agreed on, and provide specific dates and contact information (see sample letters in Resource B).

As Janet learned over the course of the project, a "no" from a business or other community organization or individual was not personal. It was not an indicator of the significance or quality of the project nor an indictment of a team member's communication skills or approach. A "no" from one organization or another simply meant that at the time of the request, a contribution of time, resources, or support was not desirable or possible. It also was an opportunity to make another contact with a different organization that could provide the resources needed.

Communicate Regularly and Widely

Janet found that regular communication with multiple stakeholders was important to the project's successful implementation. For example, the principal did not attend the team's bimonthly planning meetings. In order to keep her abreast of the team's plans and progress, Janet provided her with copies of the meeting agenda and minutes and informally discussed progress with her in the hallway or office. Initially, Janet's efforts were not acknowledged or met with much enthusiasm. Out of frustration, Janet was tempted to end the project several times, contending, "If the principal doesn't want it and can't provide any encouragement or support, why should the team continue to work so hard to implement it?" This is a natural response that arises in many schools where principal or collegial support is limited or absent. However, because Janet and the team didn't give up, remained focused on the goal of enhancing students' literacy development, and worked diligently to make the literacy project a success, the principal's support for the project and the team grew over time.

Janet and the team also found it necessary to communicate regularly with parents to publicize the project and the monthly workshops. They used two primary vehicles to communicate with parents: the school's monthly newsletter and flyers that were sent home two weeks and again two days before each workshop. Regular communication helped to keep attendance and interest high.

Team communication also was important. Through bimonthly meetings, shared minutes, and hallway conversations, the team remained focused throughout the school year. Each success solidified their excitement about and commitment to the project. Finally, communication with the community partners was important. Team members communicated with phone calls before each workshop. They sent greeting cards during the winter holidays and letters summarizing the literacy project's successes at the end of the school year. These communications were not long and cumbersome. They were short, simple interactions to thank community partners for their support and to keep them informed of how their involvement made a difference for students, parents, and teachers at the school. Communicating regularly and broadly is an important step toward developing the components of success discussed in Chapter 3.

SUMMARY

In this chapter, I provided a detailed description of a school whose readiness for comprehensive community partnerships was enhanced by the efforts of one teacher-leader. She moved her school closer to the components for successful partnerships by implementing a schoolwide project focused on a school priority; working collaboratively with school faculty, staff, and parents with whom she had built professional and personal ties; being persistent and creative when seeking community partners; and communicating regularly with key stakeholders. The vignette offered in this chapter can serve as both motivation and guide for teachers or other school leaders who would like to see more community involvement in their schools but are faced with resistance from building administrators or other colleagues.

In contrast, the following two chapters present summaries of case studies that show the success that schools can achieve when all the components described in Chapter 3 are present. The first is a case study of an urban elementary school. The second is a case study of a rural high school. These very different schools have successfully developed a variety of community partnerships that range in complexity to achieve goals for students' academic support and success. In each of the case studies, the reader will be able to see the components described in Chapter 3 in practice. Readers also will see differences in the schools' community partnerships, reflecting their different needs, resources, goals, and student populations.

5 Bringing the Community In

An Elementary School Story

In 1999, a colleague, Adia Harvey, and I conducted a case study of an elementary school member of the National Network of Partnership Schools (NNPS). The school was selected for the study based on the number and quality of its community partnerships. Data were collected over a seven-month period, from June to December. As part of the study, the school's principal and assistant principal, partnership team members, parents, students, and community partners were interviewed. Observations of community partnership activities also were conducted. Key findings of the study suggest that the school's success with its community partners was largely due to the components described in Chapter 3.

BACKGROUND

The case elementary school is one of 183 public schools serving 103,000 students in a city of approximately 600,000 residents. The school is situated in a residential and commercial section of the city. It has an enrollment of approximately 360 students in Grades K–5. The entire student population is African American. In 1999, about 10% of the students received special education services, and 79% received free or reduced-price meals. Similar numbers of students transferred in (16%) and out (17.5%) of the school in the 1998–1999 school year.

Between 1994 and 1999, the school's attendance rate surpassed the state's satisfactory standard of 94%. The school's performance on the state's standards-based exam, however, was less noteworthy. Between 1995 and

1999, the school consistently achieved a higher composite score on the exam than other schools in the district (in four of the five years, the school's composite score was nearly double the district's average). However, in 1999, the school still had fewer than 50% of its students meeting the state's satisfactory standard of 70%. The school sought to improve the academic outcomes of its students with the assistance of families and community partners.

COMMUNITY PARTNERS

During the 1998–1999 school year, the case school had ten documented community partners. Table 5.1 categorizes these partners based on those presented in Table 1.1 (see Chapter 1). As shown in Table 5.1, the case school had a variety of community partners that fell in all but five of the twelve categories identified: (a) recreational and cultural institutions, (b) military and government institutions, (c) national service and volunteer organizations, (d) sports organizations and franchises, and (e) media organizations.

These vacant categories represent community-based agencies and institutions that the school could consider for future collaborations. As also shown in Table 5.1, the school's community partnership activities were primarily student and school focused. As the case school improves its partnership program over time, it should incorporate more community-based activities that focus on students' families and the community beyond the school walls. Each of the case school's community partners is briefly described (actual names have been omitted to protect confidentiality):

1. *A nonprofit health organization.* The organization was affiliated with a school of medicine in the city. It was created to assist in the prevention of hypertension and diabetes in high-risk communities. In 1999, the organization sponsored a health awareness event that took place on the case school campus. The event included fifteen booths run by health care professionals who provided information and free screenings to participants. The organization also worked with the school to survey families about their knowledge of health care issues. In addition, the organization sponsored a good-nutrition poster competition and a healthy-cooking competition for students and their parents.

2. *A collaboration between a community-based initiative and a local church.* In collaboration with the case school, these organizations implemented an afterschool program with academic, cultural, and behavioral objectives for students. Students were assisted with homework, attended field trips, and engaged in recreational and cultural activities. The program began at 2:30 p.m. and ended at 5:15 p.m., Monday through Friday. The program had a predesigned

Table 5.1 Community Partnerships at Case Elementary School

Community Partners	Activity Focus			
	Student-centered	*Family-centered*	*School-centered*	*Community-centered*
Businesses/Corporations				
Local convenience store	x		x	
Health care agency	x		x	
Universities/Educational Institutions				
Elementary school			x	
Health Care Organizations				
Nonprofit health organization	x	x		x
Health care facility	x	x	x	
Government/Military Agencies				
National Service and Volunteer Organizations				
Faith Organizations				
Local church	x		x	
Senior Citizen Organizations				
Nursing home/rehabilitation center				x
Cultural/Recreational Institutions				
Other Community Organizations				
Nonprofit foundation			x	
A collaboration between a community-based initiative and a local church	x			
Sports Teams/Organizations				
Media Organizations				
Community Individuals				
Community volunteer	x			

parent-community involvement component. Parents or representatives, such as older siblings, grandparents, and other family members, volunteered four hours per month. The program was offered free of cost to its participants.

3. *A health care facility.* The facility provided health information to staff, students, and parents through workshops and classroom presentations. Topics included cholesterol management, HIV prevention and treatment, parenting skills, diabetes management, and CPR certification. The organization also provided refreshments for and volunteers to help implement school events, such as family fun and learning nights, father and son banquets, and end-of-year picnics. The organization also sponsored a student academic recognition program, which honored academically successful students at quarterly awards breakfasts.

4. *A nonprofit foundation.* The foundation sponsored a Hundred Book Challenge program. Participating schools were provided with rotating classroom libraries with books that were color coded by level. Teachers assessed students' reading levels and assigned them colors. Students selected books coded with these colors and read, in class, thirty minutes each day. Students also were encouraged to take books home and read to their parents. Every book that the child read was recorded. After a certain number were read, children received incentives and rewards, such as pens and pencils. Students who read 100 books or more were recognized at the school's quarterly awards breakfasts.

5. *A suburban elementary school.* The PTA at this elementary school provided the case school with books for over two years. The partner school also shared with the case school a book credit that allowed the school to purchase new books from Scholastic Press. The school formally adopted the case school during the 1999–2000 school year to expand their exchange and interaction.

6. *A health care agency.* The agency had a community outreach initiative—Partnership in Education Program—that included forty-two volunteers who worked with three schools. Seven volunteers from this agency supported the case school in a variety of ways. They acted as tutors for students with academic problems. They also held book drives for the school. During the 1998–1999 school year, the agency donated 600 books to the school. The agency also donated several computers that were used in the school's computer center.

7. *A local church.* The church had an outreach committee that provided school supplies to students in need and also provided refreshments

for school parties, including Valentine's Day and Christmas parties. Members of the outreach committee also worked as volunteers in the student cafeteria.

8. *A local convenience store.* The manager of the store sponsored recreational and crafts activities for students on Children's Day, which was held on the school campus. He also volunteered in classrooms and sat on school committees, including the PTSA, as a community representative.

9. *A nursing home and rehabilitation center.* The center housed 200 patients on five floors. Students provided residents with cards, decorations, and entertainment on holidays, including Christmas, Valentine's Day, and Thanksgiving. Students decorated the main hall of the building as well as residents' rooms. They also visited and lunched with residents.

10. *A community member.* The community member was an employee at the state's poison center. He regularly volunteered at the school to talk to students about poison prevention. He also provided students with educational materials that emphasized the importance of "poison proofing" their environments.

As of June 1999, each of these community partners had been collaborating with the school for at least two years. Some of the partnerships were initiated by the school through personal contacts or requests to the organizations' outreach coordinators. This was the case for the partnerships with the elementary school, health care agency, convenience store, and nursing home. Other partnerships were initiated by organizations and individuals in the community, such as the collaborations with the nonprofit health organization, the health care facility, the local church, and the community member. Still others of these partnerships were a result of the school applying for participation in projects such as the afterschool program and the Hundred Book Challenge program.

Regardless of who initiated contact (the school and community partners reported that they were equally comfortable with either party initiating contact), a variety of factors allowed the school to attract and sustain these partnerships over time.

COMMITMENT TO STUDENTS' LEARNING

One of the factors that community partners found attractive about the case school was its high commitment to students' learning. Here, I describe ways in which this commitment was manifested and perceived by students, faculty, parents, and community partners.

Learning as a School Priority

The principal of the case school was committed to creating an academically rigorous and supportive learning environment for students and was deliberate in her actions to achieve this goal. She worked diligently to ensure that teachers had the instructional materials and support that they needed to be "focused and ready to do their job and fulfill their responsibilities." She also worked hard to ensure that teachers worked in a secure, well-maintained, and orderly environment. She stated,

> I make sure that the building is safe, and that everyone who works here, including cafeteria workers and custodians, works together like a well-oiled machine. . . . Bills are paid, people get along, and in case of emergencies or crises, I am here to intervene.

The co-chair of the Action Team for Partnerships who also was a third-grade teacher described the principal as "wonderfully organized" and committed to students' success.

According to the students and parents interviewed for the study, the principal's goal of creating a challenging and supportive learning environment was being realized. When randomly selected students in Grades 3–5 were asked whether they believed that the school was good, the overwhelming response was "yes." Students explained that what made the school good was that the principal and teachers cared about students' learning. A fourth-grade student explained that what he liked most about the school was the class work that his teacher assigned and how she helped him to understand the lessons. When a fifth-grade student was asked what was good about the teachers at the school, she responded, "They help all the children learn."

The parents of these students also described the school's commitment to learning as its most outstanding feature; and when asked to rate the school on a scale from *poor* (1) to *excellent* (5), each parent interviewed rated the school either as *very good* (4) or as *excellent* (5). When asked to explain her rating of the school, one parent noted that teachers at the school were always willing to work with parents to encourage students' academic growth. She said, "The teachers will let you know exactly what your child is doing; they'll call you at work or wherever, and tell you how your child is doing and how you can help. I like that." Another parent stated that her daughter's first-grade teacher was "excellent in getting the students started in reading and in disciplining them." She also commented on the importance of the school's parent workshops that focused on students' learning. When discussing their impact she stated, "They helped me get back involved with my kids and helped me to realize how important my involvement was for my kids' success."

Parents who were interviewed were aware and appreciative of academically focused activities at the school, such as the Hundred Book Challenge and the afterschool programs. Each of the parents interviewed indicated that they were kept aware of school activities and the community partners involved in the school through conversations with their children, attendance at school meetings and events, and the school's monthly newsletters. Two of the parents worked full-time outside the home and commented that the school newsletter was an especially important source of information for them when they could not come to the school building. Students identified the many books in the classrooms and library, the volunteers who come to the school to read to them as part of the school's Hundred Book Challenge program, and their computer class as the best things about the school in addition to the principal and classroom teachers.

Community Response to School's Commitment

According to its community partners, the school's visible commitment to students' learning was one of the key factors that attracted them to the school and kept them involved. The community partner at the elementary school stated,

> Just from phone calls and talks with the PTA, we've gotten the impression that the staff . . . [at the school] is extremely committed to raising students' test scores. They are doing everything that they can to improve their reading levels. . . . This commitment helps the program along. You've got a committed faculty, and students are doing better and better.

The community partner at the health care facility was impressed by the level of family involvement in the school's efforts to improve student learning. Based on her attendance at school events, such as the academic recognition breakfasts, the respondent commented,

> The one thing that I love is the parent support. It's not there for everybody, but it's there. For students whose parents cannot be in the building, maybe their friend's mother is there to give them a hug. Parents come and take pictures. It's wonderful.

Community partners believed that through their contributions, they were helping the school to provide a richer learning environment for students. The respondent at the nonprofit foundation explained that they continued to collaborate with the case school to assist it in improving students' reading. She observed,

> I have a stack of notes from students about the program . . . and that's terrific. It's helpful to the school, too. . . . We're interested in students' feedback so that we can improve our efforts and help the school to improve its efforts.

When discussing why the health care facility's relationship with the case school had intensified over time, the respondent stated, "I have seen a difference since we started. When we first began our awards breakfasts, we started with about fifteen students and their parents; now each quarter, we have nearly 300 people in attendance!"

The case school, although not the highest performing school in the district, was viewed as effective. This feature of the school was clearly linked to its success in attracting committed community partners to assist it in its school improvement efforts. Community partners wanted to be a part of an effective school that was visibly focused on students' learning. A second factor that emerged as significant in its ability to attract and sustain community partners was the principal's support and vision for community involvement.

PRINCIPAL LEADERSHIP

Principal leadership and support for partnerships helped the case school to develop meaningful community connections. In June, when the case study began, the school was experiencing a transition. The principal of the school since 1995 was leaving to assume a district-level position. He was active during the summer, however, as the school's assistant principal since 1997 prepared to become the school's new head administrator. Based on school observations and interviews with parents, students, Action Team co-chairs, community partners, and the principals themselves, the transition process was smooth and almost imperceptible. The smooth transition was largely due to the principals' shared belief in and support for school, family, and community partnerships as strategies for school improvement.

Principals' Views on Community Involvement

The outgoing principal did not make a sharp distinction between family and community involvement. Instead he viewed the school, family, and community as a seamless web of supports and resources for students' learning. He stated,

> Part of the parent component is the community component, because we are all products of the communities out of which we come. . . . I really wish we didn't have schools. I wish we would take kids out in the community and we'd learn everything out there.

The current principal makes a distinction between family and community involvement. Although she sees both as crucial to students' learning, she views parent involvement as primary and community involvement as supplemental. She explained,

> The real magic is in parents. It is their presence and approval; if you ask anyone who has done any teaching, that makes the difference. . . . When children know that their parents are interested, the students just do so much better. It doesn't have to be mom or dad, but someone from home—it just makes a world of difference for them as far as their behavior, as well as academics.
>
>   There is a role for the community as well. . . . It may be secondary, but it certainly is wanted and appreciated. Community involvement lets our children know that there are other people in the community who care about them, people who are willing to work with them and do things for them.

Although their views differed, both principals valued the role of family and community involvement in the educational process. Their beliefs translated into open and responsive attitudes toward opportunities for school-community collaboration and actions that reflected these attitudes. According to the current principal, who once questioned her ability to "network" with community groups to solicit support for the school,

> If I find a group or an individual who is ready to do something, I am ready to tap into it. . . . We are always willing to accept things and find people to do things for our children and make our children aware that someone is doing something special for them.

Community Response to Principal Leadership

Each of the community partners described the current and former school principals as supportive of community involvement. It was this support that, in many cases, explained their ongoing partnerships with the case school and not with others in the immediate area. The community partner from the health care facility stated,

> I don't want to pinpoint any schools, but I've gone into some and have been totally turned off by the administration. If I'm turned off, what's the interest in helping you, if you can't be civil or nice to me?

The same community partner praised the case school's former and current principals for their openness to community involvement. When speaking about the school leadership, she commented that at the case school, the administrator had "always been open to anything that will help kids and the school." She continued, "I can't speak highly enough of him, and the assistant principal is really nice, too." A third factor that was linked to the school's successful community outreach was the work of its ATP.

ACTION TEAM FOR PARTNERSHIPS

The nonprofit foundation partner agreed that the principal was important to the initial development of successful community collaborations. However, recognizing the many responsibilities of the principal, she also contended that it was important for the principal to build the capacity of others in the school to maintain the partnerships. She explained,

> The principal's involvement in the initial stages of partnership development is crucial. Up front, we want a commitment by the principal. The principal also needs to designate somebody who's going to be accountable for the relationship and for the program in the school.

Both the former and current principals have used the school's ATP to build the capacity of others to facilitate partnership program development. The co-chairs of the school's action team stated that the principal supports the team in many ways. The current principal was a member of the ATP for two years and was actively involved in writing the school's annual partnership plan, a key part of the its school improvement plan. She ensured that the team co-chairs regularly reported the team's progress at school improvement meetings, and perhaps most important, she provided coverage for classrooms so that ATP members could meet every month. Regularly scheduled meetings helped the school to overcome one of the most common challenges that schools face when developing partnership programs—finding time to meet.

Although both ATP co-chairs were pleased with the school's community partnerships, they looked forward to expanding and improving them. Both agreed that with the principal's continued support, the district's continued emphasis on family and community involvement as a strategy for school improvement, and ongoing professional development on the topic, the school's partnership efforts would thrive. The school's focus on students' learning, principal support for community involvement, and its active ATP opened the doors to community partners. However, what kept partners at the school once they entered were the school's climate and its capacity for open communication.

WELCOMING SCHOOL CLIMATE

Parents, teachers, students, and community members agreed that the case school was warm, friendly, and welcoming. It embodied the *community school* concept as described by the current principal:

> This is really a community school. People always say, "You all don't ever go home." For a small school, we have long hours. We're here usually from 6:30 a.m. until 7:30 p.m. every day. There are teachers and parents here. . . . They come here for meetings, and other community organizations use our grounds, or our parking lots, or our building to have meetings on the weekends. . . . I think that it is crucial and is what makes . . . the school what it is.

The principal worked to convey this conception of the school to her staff. She stated,

> I've said to my staff, and I think that this is so, most parents, and I would imagine members of the community, are afraid of the unknown. . . . I think that they are weary of coming into schoolhouses where they don't feel welcome. That is the first key, that people are made to feel welcomed.

The principal's emphasis on creating a welcoming, friendly environment resonated with her staff. The community member who volunteered at the school observed that everyone in the school, from the secretary to the principal, had a welcoming attitude that was engaging. He stated, "I can honestly say that I have had good contacts with everybody that I have met at the school." The health care facility volunteer stated,

> It is definitely . . . [the school's] spirit that is special. . . . I noticed that when I take other volunteers with me, they can't wait to get back to [the school]. . . . It's something about that school that really draws you to it.

The co-chair of the ATP, who is a kindergarten teacher, stated,

> This is a friendly school, where teachers and the administration work together and the parents and community are involved. . . . Everyone seems to get along, and everyone is involved and helpful to one another. . . . It's just a nice place to be.

This sense of community within the case school's walls facilitated effective partnering with community agencies and organizations outside its walls.

Community Response to School Climate

The health care facility partner described the reception that she received at the case school in the following way: "I was wondering how I would be received, and it's been wonderful. The kids, they hug me, they love me, and I love them." The local church partner also found the school's openness and receptivity critical to the partnership's success. She noted that many schools are often "leery" of church partners. "Schools shouldn't be frightened of people coming from a church," she said. "When we go to a school, we're going there to assist or do whatever we can for the school. We're not going to convert students." Both these partners had attempted to initiate collaborations with another school in the area but did not follow through because they were not met with the reception found at the case school.

The community partners also found the case school to be appreciative of community involvement. Although they stated that formal acknowledgment was not necessary, the community partners were impressed by the case school's expressions of gratitude. Several of the partners reported receiving thank you letters and notes from students; some reported having been thanked for their assistance over the intercom system; others reported having been stopped on the street by students and their parents and thanked for their service; many reported having been acknowledged in the school's newsletter; and still others reported having received certificates of appreciation at the school's end-of-year awards ceremony. However, the community partners agreed with the statement made by the nonprofit foundation partner: "Our acknowledgment," she said, "is in the results for the students. That's what we have our eye on."

TWO-WAY COMMUNICATION

Last, the former and current principals, ATP co-chairs, and community businesses and organizations emphasized the importance of two-way communication for the success of the school's community collaborations. Such communication is necessary to determine the most suitable kinds of involvement and to clarify the roles and responsibilities of each partner. According the former principal,

> Sometimes a community partner's ideas might not necessarily fit in with the school goals, and therefore we have to help them. We have to work together to find out the best way to partner. I have found that often people come in with ideas about what they'd like to do, and what I try to do is take them on a tour of the school. They have a chance to see the students, to see the concerns that we have, and to see the strengths and weaknesses that we have. This helps to shape their ideas, and then we can talk about possible partnership activities.

The current principal emphasized the importance of honesty in communications with community partners and potential partners so that each party is fully aware of the intent and expectations of the other. She found that initial honest and up-front conversations prevent both parties from wasting each other's time. The principal used a simple measure to determine if a community partnership program was right for the school: whether the partnership would be positive for the students.

Community partners also emphasized the importance of honest, open dialogue in which the school expressed its needs and the community partners expressed what they could offer. All community partners agreed that it was not important who initiated the dialogue but that the dialogue occurred. Without such dialogue, the local church partner noted, "We have no idea what the school needs, and the school has no idea what we have to offer." "It is important to allow people to come in," she continued, "and sit and talk" to determine if a partnership is possible. The nonprofit health organization partner stated, "Our main goal is working with other groups and organizations and seeing where they are. Once we evaluate their needs, we can determine what it is that we can do to help them." The manager of the local convenience store also emphasized the importance of open, two-way communication:

> I'm a relational person. I like to sit down and talk. I like to know what is going on with the school and what type of help is needed. I don't want to come in and dictate anything. . . . I also don't want anyone to tell me, "This is what we are doing, get on board or get out." That to me is the biggest turnoff. What is important is dialogue.

Open, two-way communication also was identified as playing a major role in helping partnerships to grow, improve, and intensify over time. As the school's needs changed, both the former and current school principals reported having discussed these changes with current and potential partners so that their involvement could evolve in complementary ways or come to appropriate conclusions. Community partners, in turn, were encouraged to communicate with the school when their foci, resources, or capabilities changed so that their collaborations with the school continued to be positive. One community partner reported scheduling meetings with the school whenever the administration changed, "to see what . . . [the new principal's] needs are and how we can best assist them." Open, two-way communication helped the school to avoid conflicts that might otherwise have threatened the viability of the partnerships.

This was the case with the school's afterschool program. When school faculty found items missing from their rooms after the rooms were used for the program, they discussed their concerns with program leaders. The leaders then began to better monitor students participating in the program. The end result was positive for all the parties involved and helped the program in its efforts to "keep trying to improve."

SUMMARY

The case study revealed five factors that supported one urban school's ability to develop and maintain meaningful community partnerships. These factors were (a) a commitment to students' learning; (b) principal leadership; (c) an active ATP; (d) a welcoming school climate; and (e) two-way communication about the levels and kinds of community involvement. These factors, along with the district support that the case school received, correspond to the components of partnership success described in Chapter 3 and created fertile ground in which school-community partnerships flourished.

As a result of these partnerships, the school had computers that students loved to use; classrooms and a library full of books; an incentive program for honor-roll students; an afterschool program; financial support for partnership activities and events; community speakers for parent workshops; and relationships with community businesses, organizations, and individuals that brought the school and its community partners a great deal of satisfaction. Thus these partnerships supported the school's efforts to provide a challenging and nurturing learning environment for its students. This kind of support is important for school improvement, especially for schools in high-risk, urban communities that are increasingly asked to improve students' academic and behavioral outcomes, often without the necessary increases in material and human resources.

Community partnerships, however, are not important only for schools in urban areas. Schools in suburban and rural areas also benefit from community outreach and support. The following chapter illustrates the importance for one rural high school whose community links have been critical to its effectiveness.

6 Creating Closer Community Ties

A High School Study

Between October and December of 2002, a colleague, Karla Lewis, and I conducted case studies of three high school members of the National Network of Partnership Schools (NNPS).[10] Potential sites were limited to those whose evaluations of their partnership program quality on NNPS annual surveys ranged from good to excellent on a five-point scale for at least two consecutive years prior to the start of the study. Five of the seventy-five high schools that were members of NNPS at the time of the study met this criterion. Final sites were chosen to reflect different community contexts and school demographics. One of these sites was located in a rural county in a midwestern state. This chapter describes community partnerships in this county, focusing specifically on activities implemented at Rural High. (Again, pseudonyms are used to ensure participants' anonymity and confidentiality.) The description is crafted to shed light on the components for successful community partnerships introduced in Chapter 3.

BACKGROUND

The District

Five schools—three elementary schools, one junior high school, and one high school—compose the Waterford County school district. Because of the district's size, the parent involvement coordinator who helped to develop the district's partnership team in 1998 decided that it would be more efficient and unifying to create one districtwide partnership committee rather than five school-based teams. According to Cheryl Finn, the former district parent involvement coordinator, currently an elementary school principal as well as a district partnership committee member,

> I know that sometimes some buildings might think that it is taking from their individuality, but a solid, working, well-defined districtwide partnership plan works better for us than trying to do it at different buildings.

While small, the district is made up of three separate villages. To bring the district's disparate populations closer together, primary goals of the district partnership committee were to increase student involvement in community outreach projects and community involvement in students' learning and development. Partnership activities involving elementary schools included a community mentoring program in which community volunteers were trained by school faculty to tutor K–5 students who needed individual attention in reading and a hand-washing experiment in which a local health center partnered with district second graders to determine the effects of correct hand-washing procedures on the presence and growth of bacteria. Several businesses also supported the district's newsletter through advertisements and provided student and family incentives at school events. The district's success with its partnership efforts led to a state award for community involvement in educational improvement.

The district's partnership committee meets monthly and is made up of faculty, family, and community representatives from each school. Phillip Brussels, who has been a member since its inception, described the committee as follows: "I think it is a very friendly group . . . a very open group and very easy to get along with, not a bunch of snooty people." The committee's president, James Fence, attributes the success of the team to its committed members, who primarily were recruited through direct requests. According to Mr. Fence, "The one-on-one request seems to be best at getting people interested; they see what accomplishments that you have had. I would say that is about it, the one-on-one."

The president also attributed the team's success to the support provided by district educational leaders. He commented, "[We] do our part but then we have the administration that is very active in helping us with partnerships with businesses and so forth in the district." Ms. Finn also shared this view of the importance of district support:

The most important thing to any community partnership, I think, is the buy-in of administration. If the superintendent and school board members buy into a program, it makes it so much easier for you. You don't have to follow through with red tape as far as formal meetings and going before the Board of Education to get things enacted. Things move a lot smoother just because of the time frame and if you have administrators that go to the meetings and who say, "That is a wonderful idea, go for it." They take it back and present it before the Board of Education.

Last, Mr. Fence attributed the team's success and longevity (it's been active for seven years) to the optimism and focus with which members have approached the team's work:

The main thing is to go in and try to work with a positive attitude. Every place has negatives; you might try to eliminate it, but you can't dwell on it. Just go for the positives; keep asking yourself, "What can I do to make the education of our kids better?"

The High School

We believe in the innate value of every human life, and we recognize that an effective educational process must nurture and develop the whole person. A caring and supportive school environment produces a feeling of trust among students, teachers, parents, administrators, and community in partnership. Every student will leave . . . [the high school] with a strong sense of self-worth, a healthy respect for the rights of individuals, and a determined commitment to life-long learning as a productive, responsible member of society. (High School Vision Statement)

Rural High draws its approximately 680 students from all three villages that compose the Waterford County school district. The high school's student population is predominantly European American (96%). At the time of the study, nearly one quarter of these students received free- or reduced-price meals (see Table 6.1). Students were offered courses in ten departments: (a) Business, (b) English, (c) Fine Arts, (d) Foreign Language, (e) Health/ Physical Education, (f) Mathematics, (g) Science, (h) Social Studies, (i) Special Services, and (j) Vocation.

The mustard-yellow high school is about thirty years old and needs renovation and additional space, as evidenced by the eight temporary portables that flank the main building. Portables were needed to accommodate the

Table 6.1   School Demographics

	Rural High School
Number of Students	660
Black	4%
White	96%
Other	<1%
Student ADA*	95%
Number receiving FARM**	24%+
Number of Faculty	42
Student/Teacher Ratio	15.7:1
Teacher DAR***	96%

SOURCE: *National Center for Education Statistics,* (n.d.), 2000–2001 school year.
*ADA: Average daily attendance; source: respective state departments of education
**FARM: Free and reduced-price meals
***DAR: Daily attendance rate

growing number of students that resulted from the consolidation of high schools in the county in 1993. Due to lack of space, high school students shared a cafeteria with young students in a nearby elementary school.

Working within these constraints, the school has made significant changes to provide students with the facilities and resources they need to compete in educational and workplace settings that are increasingly technology dependent. The cafeteria, for example, was fashioned into a multimedia classroom (satellite links, videos, televisions, etc.), computer classroom, computer lab, and vending room. The computer classroom has the latest Macintosh computers with seventeen-inch screens and a new server. The computer lab has older computers, but they are still less than five years old. Much of the equipment has been acquired through grants and community contributions that have been coordinated by the district's partnership team and the school's principal. Based on increasing standardized test scores, the school's efforts have paid off. According to the principal, "The success of our kids, in terms of going on to school, being successful, moving on, and also our school's success as reflected in our state report card and so forth has been outstanding."

PRINCIPAL LEADERSHIP

The district's partnership committee was established before Albert Harrison became principal of Rural High. However, convinced of its importance for schools and the significance of its goals for students and the surrounding community, the principal has supported the committee's work. Faculty and students from the high school are members of the committee. Mr. Harrison viewed his role as that of a facilitator. He noted,

> [Rural High] is the single most visible entity in the community. What happens at the high school—good, bad, or indifferent—is sort of representative of what happens in the community. I think that we have tried to be proactive and tried to locate or identify the needs of our community and the needs of our students and tried to service them the best we could. . . . As principal of the high school, I try to make things happen as the facilitator of things that the teachers want to see happen, that the students what to see happen, that parents want to see happen. I am very much involved in that facilitating role.

He also acknowledged the importance of having a partnership committee with which to work. He commented, "You have to have a team. You have to work together as a team. Nobody can accomplish anything by themselves." The principal has helped to facilitate a number of community partnership activities at the school. Many of these activities, as described later in the chapter, are focused on providing services and resources to the surrounding community. The principal viewed the purpose of these activities as being twofold. While they provided community services, they also supported students' well-being, a central focus of the school and the district.

A STUDENT FOCUS

Rural High's students have been central to the district's partnership efforts. As members of the district's partnership team, student leaders have helped to plan and implement partnership activities conducted in the district. According to Mr. Brussels, the district partnership activities have helped to bring the school's adolescents closer to the community:

> The kids must understand that the community does like them and that they are willing to help out. If they know that the community is willing to help out, then possibly those children, when they graduate,

are going to be more willing to come back and help add to the community. It is that sense of family that is very important.

The principal further contended that Rural High's student involvement in the district's partnership activities helped to close the generation gap between the district's elderly members and its teenagers.

I think that [senior citizens] may look at our students with a little bit of fear or mistrust or whatever, but I think that whenever they talk to the kids and are around the kids and so forth, it helps that relationship, which is an important part of the community.

The social capital gained by students through their involvement and interaction with adults in the community is viewed as positively affecting students' self-concepts. According to Ms. Finn,

Every kid wants the same thing. They want to know that they are important and that you value what they do. It is just what everybody is about and sometimes our high school kids just miss out on that. When you spend many hours with them, you know that is what our community activities provide these kids.

To celebrate students' efforts, Rural High, along with the partnership committee, has established a scholarship program for graduating seniors. The principal explained,

We pay attention to students who do community service. We offer a scholarship every year, the biggest criterion for that is somebody who goes out within the community and volunteers their time.

COMMUNITY PARTNERS AND ACTIVITIES

Well, I think that a successful partnership is when both people, both groups, both agencies, whatever the case might be, benefit by the relationship. I think in any successful relationship or partnership, both sides benefit. (Albert Harrison, Rural High's Principal)

The district had nearly twenty active community partners. Rural High's community partnerships represented all but two of the categories introduced in Chapter 1. Table 6.2 shows a full account of these partnerships. These partnerships are highlighted to illustrate the school-community connections that have existed in this small rural high school.

Table 6.2 Community Partners Active at Rural High

Possible Community Partners	Rural High Partnerships
Business/Corporations: Local businesses, national corporations and franchises	Providing student internships, refreshments for school events, student/family incentives
Universities and Educational Institutions: Colleges, universities, high schools, and other educational institutions	High school students tutoring at local elementary schools
Health Care Organizations: Hospitals, health care centers, mental health facilities, health departments, health foundations and associations	Hospitals cosponsoring community health fair
Government and Military Agencies: Fire departments, police departments, chamber of commerce, city council, other local and state government agencies and departments	Health Dept., Fire Dept., City Council, Fire Dept. Police/Sheriff Dept. acting as volunteers and guest speakers for school programs
National Service and Volunteer Organizations: Rotary Club, Lions Club, Kiwanis Club, VISTA, Concerned Black Men, Inc., Shriners, Boy and Girl Scouts, YWCA, United Way, AmeriCorps, Urban League	Students supporting United Way through fundraising

Organization	Activity
Faith Organizations: Churches, mosques, synagogues, other religious organizations and charities	Students collecting canned food and volunteering at a shelter organized by faith organizations
Senior Citizens Organizations: Nursing homes, senior volunteer and service organizations	Students organizing social events for senior organizations
Cultural and Recreational Institutions: Zoos, museums, libraries, recreational centers, sports teams/orgs	Library assisting in organizing school events (e.g., book drive)
Media: Local newspapers, radio stations, cable networks	Helping to disseminate information about Health Fair
Sports Teams: Minor and major league sports teams, NBA, NCAA, etc.	_____
Other Organizations: Fraternities, sororities, foundations, neighborhood associations (political, alumni, etc.)	_____
Community Individuals: Individual volunteers from the surrounding school community	Supporting health fair and other school events

Community Health Fair

The Community Health Fair was one of the district's most successful community partnerships. The fair began with about 100 participants and became an annual event of over 500 participants. Since its inception, the fair has been held on Rural High's football field.

Several community organizations have partnered with the high school and district to ensure the event's success. A hospital, a local health care facility, and the county health department have provided free screenings for cancer, body fat, blood pressure, blood glucose, and other health concerns; flu shots; and health information. A local radio station has provided free advertisements for the fair. Rural High students and other community volunteers have operated the arts and crafts booths, offering free face painting, balloons, and treats for younger children. The local library has organized book drives and book readings. The school district's venture capital grant has provided funds for food.

Recently, the Health Fair has been immediately followed by the high school's Back to School Rally, in which parents, students, and faculty meet and greet one another and exchange important information about the upcoming school year. For this event, Rural High has partnered with a local stationery store to provide free school supplies for students.

Urban Mission

The district partnership team helped to coordinate a partnership between Rural High and a shelter, the Urban Mission, supported by local churches. Rural High students have volunteered at the shelter, collected canned goods, and helped to prepare and serve food at the shelter. When describing the project, Mr. Harrison explained,

> Students going down to . . . [Urban Mission] and working in a soup kitchen, I suppose, might make some parents nervous because of what they might be exposed to. We have decided that it's an opportunity that our students need.

Internship Program

Through its work with the district partnership team, Rural High School also has developed a successful internship program that has allowed high school students to gain real work experience in a variety of professions, including health care and veterinary medicines. Moreover, the program has allowed students to develop meaningful relationships with professionals and business leaders in the community.

When discussing the benefits of community involvement at Rural High, the principal commented,

> They lead to a certain trust by the community in what happens at the high school. That is what we are all looking to accomplish—trust and a good positive relationship between school and community.

District and school leaders have hoped that closer ties between schools and the community would provide the support needed to ensure adequate funding for educational improvement. Indeed, district leaders suggested that without strong school-community connections, legislation to increase educational spending in the district would surely fail, and needed renovations and upgrades would not occur.

SUMMARY

Rural communities and school districts are generally smaller than urban and suburban districts, with fewer businesses and community-based organizations. This environment is sometimes viewed as challenging by educational leaders who seek to develop comprehensive community partnerships. Waterford County illustrates how a team approach to community partnerships can be developed to accommodate a variety of settings and goals.

Waterford County's decision to create one district committee to collaboratively plan and coordinate community partnerships for each of its five schools reduced competition for partners. Moreover, Waterford's approach allowed schools to coordinate activities to better accommodate the busy schedules of parents and community volunteers, thereby increasing participation across events.

The approach also created the space for dialogue about districtwide needs and goals that spanned grade levels, positions, and perspectives. Finally, it facilitated the engagement of the district's superintendent and school board. While monthly visits at separate schools may have been difficult to accommodate, the superintendent was able to attend the partnership committee's monthly meetings or send a representative.

Despite the uniqueness of Waterford, and indeed any school and district, the components for success discussed in Chapter 3 were present: (a) a high-functioning school, (b) a student-centered environment, (c) an effective partnership team, (d) principal leadership, and (e) external support. Despite its limited space, Rural High was an organized, effective, and student-centered learning environment with a principal who supported and facilitated community partnerships. Furthermore, Waterford's partnership team was well functioning and had the support of the district's superintendent and school board. With these components in place, Waterford has had award-winning success with its community partnerships. The following chapter describes additional goal-oriented partnership activities implemented in a variety of K–12 schools in the United States.

7 Promising Practices for Community Partnerships

Many schools are developing community partnerships to achieve important goals. Previous chapters have shown the importance of five components: (a) a high level of school functioning, (b) a student-centered environment, (c) an effective partnership team, (d) principal leadership, and (e) external support for the successful implementation of a comprehensive array of community partnerships. Activities showcased in this chapter highlight the creativity that also is present in promising community partnership practices. Creativity is important because it helps schools to shape and mold what they have into what they need to reach important goals for school improvement and students' success.

Activities described in this chapter are selected from Promising Partnership Practices (Salinas & Jansorn, 2000, 2001, 2002, 2003, 2004), an annual publication of the National Network of Partnership Schools (NNPS);[11] the year of publication is indicated in parentheses for each activity. These twelve activities include a wide variety of community partners and have been implemented to achieve a broad spectrum of goals. The elementary, middle, and high schools implementing these activities are located in urban, suburban, and rural communities serving diverse student populations. What they have in common is their commitment to finding innovative ways to strengthen their students' schools, families, and communities.

ACTIVITY 1: GOAL—IMPROVE READING (2004)

Banyan Elementary School's Reading Mentoring Program began when a high school student approached the principal, asking to tutor third graders. She recruited forty of her classmates from St. Brendan High School and offered to start a weekly reading tutorial with forty-two third graders experiencing reading difficulties.

The St. Brendan High student coordinator met and trained the mentors on a regular basis and wrote monthly lesson plans for the students. The mentors went above and beyond the call of normal tutoring: They dressed up in costumes and read folk tales from different countries, planted flowers in Banyan's butterfly garden, and made valentines in February with the Banyan students. Tutors hoped to raise student achievement and minimize third-grade retention. They felt that one-on-one tutoring would help to advance these goals.

The tutorial program cost $1,000 to implement and was funded through the Governor's Mentoring Initiative. Businesses such as the state lottery and Comcast provided program support as well. The school publicized the tutorial program through weekly newsletters, fliers, posters, and the state department of education's Web site.

Both high school students and third graders benefited from the program. Many of the third graders were learning English as a second language and needed extra help to move beyond Level 1 in reading. After being a part of the program, all of these students increased their reading scores on two required standardized exams. In addition, the high school students found enjoyment and satisfaction in their work. In an article for the state department of education's newsletter, one teen mentor commented, "I love working with kids, so this was an awesome experience for me. I see how the kids have improved their reading, and that gives me a great feeling of success!" The partnership between Banyan Elementary School and St. Brendan High School has been well received by families, students, and staff at both schools. Inspired by the reading mentoring program's success, the schools have partnered for science fairs and other student activities. The reading program plans to expand to support more students in upcoming school years.

ACTIVITY 2: GOAL—IMPROVE MATH SKILLS (2003)

Kennedy Junior High School (KJHS) has a business partnership with Jackson Moving Services. As a result of this partnership, the sixth-grade math teacher provided students with the opportunity for "quality work in the math curriculum through the application of estimation skills, while calculating volume and weight in a real-world situation." Beat Pete: An Estimation Project afforded students the opportunity to provide customers with estimates for their moving jobs.

Beat Pete was a daylong activity in which students went with Pete Nechi, a Jackson Moving Services salesperson, to see his clients. In 2001, he was named the "Most Accurate Estimator" out of more than 2,000 salespeople. In 2002 and 2003, he finished second. Students played Beat Pete, in which they tried to provide the most accurate weight and cost estimations for several moving jobs. Students who estimated nearest to the weight of the shipment and the final costs were awarded prizes. The project demonstrated real-world applications of classroom lessons and proved how important it is to prepare accurate estimates.

To start organizing the project, Jackson Moving Services found customers willing to allow students in their homes. This was the greatest challenge to this activity. However, many families were willing to participate after being assured that students would adhere to house rules, such as no shoes and no food. Next, KJHS arranged bus transportation and parent permission. KJHS Home & School paid for the bus and for a substitute teacher for the math teacher's other classes. As a final preplanning step, students received printed materials regarding the day's activities.

According to an internal evaluation performed by KJHS administration and faculty, Beat Pete was a great success. Students were able to participate in a concrete activity that answered the age-old question, "Why do I need to learn math in school?" Students also were exposed to moving services as a potential career choice. In the future, KJHS plans to explore ways to allow a greater number of students to participate.

ACTIVITY 3: GOAL—INCREASE STUDENTS' AWARENESS OF CAREER OPPORTUNITIES (2001)

Career Week 2001 at Arlington Elementary School increased students' interest in and knowledge of diverse career options. The event was an innovative way to improve relationships with business partners and collaborate with neighboring communities.

A school team consisting of teachers and parents worked diligently to locate and invite professionals from a variety of occupations. Through letters, phone calls, and personal contacts, the committee secured the following speakers: an architect, a dentist, a police officer, a beautician, a computer programmer, a caterer, a certified public accountant, an occupational therapist, a bus driver, a photojournalist, a mortician, an engineer, a pediatrician, a social worker, and representatives from other areas of employment.

Once the guest speakers were confirmed, the team assigned them to classrooms, based on students' interests. To prepare for the guest speaker's presentations, students researched the occupation and generated questions. After the presentations, students extended their learning by writing essays about what occupations they wanted to pursue. They also wrote thank you notes to Career Week visitors.

Funds from the school paid for Career Week. The guests enjoyed a continental breakfast each morning. Guests also received gift packs with the school's mission statement and goals, a school pen, and a certificate of participation.

The students, teachers, and parents of Arlington were pleased with the visitors and the wealth of information and insights that they shared. A number of participants volunteered to serve as mentors to those students who expressed an interest in their particular fields. Many of the career professionals enjoyed the experience so much that they readily agreed to come back for Career Week 2002.

ACTIVITY 4: GOAL—IMPROVE NINTH-GRADE PERFORMANCE ON STATE PROFICIENCY EXAM (2002)

James Ford Rhodes High School wanted to increase the number of ninth-grade students passing the Ohio proficiency test. The school recruited community and teacher volunteers to tutor students after school. The school sent flyers to education departments of local colleges inviting students to an open house in October. College students attending the open house learned about the tutoring program and agreed to tutor students as part of their community service. Retired educators, grandparents, and parent alumni also offered tutoring assistance.

Tutoring sessions ran three times per week from 2:30 to 4:30 p.m. until May. All participating ninth graders had their own tutors. The tutors used proficiency materials and workbooks focused on fractions, division, and word problems.

Committed guidance counselors, teachers, college students, and interested parents took struggling students under their wings. Out of 500 ninth graders, 100 received tutoring. Student test scores on the proficiency test increased from October to March. Specifically, reading scores increased 7%, writing scores increased 18%, and math scores rose 18%. Increasing test scores on the ninth-grade proficiency test continues to be a goal. Thanks to the volunteer efforts of college students, retired teachers, grandparents, and parent alumni, Rhodes High School is on the road to success.

ACTIVITY 5: GOAL— IMPROVE STUDENT WRITING AND TECHNOLOGY SKILLS (2002)

The Buddy Reading Program between North Central College and Mill Street Elementary School involved approximately sixty preservice education students and sixty fourth graders and fifth graders who engaged in a one-to-one dialogue about specific novels. Communication occurred via a college-based WEBboard that allowed students to exchange ideas and make connections using the latest computer technology. The program's goals for students were twofold: (a) to participate in a learning dialogue about grade-appropriate literature and (b) to learn about and use technology as a tool of communication.

Twice a week for three weeks, the fourth and fifth graders engaged in written discussions via the WEBboard with their college reading buddies. Mill Street Elementary School students enhanced their reading comprehension skills by making predictions and connections and holding meaningful discussions about the novels with their college reading buddies. The North Central College students incorporated reading strategies from their methods classes and from Mill Street teachers in their Web-based discussions and face-to-face meetings with students.

Fourth graders and their college buddies read *Yang the Youngest*, *Junebug*, and *Jackie Robinson*, while fifth graders and their college buddies read *Pigs Might Fly*, *Harry's Mad*, and *Martin's Mice*. All novels were part of the district curriculum. A subcommittee of the Literacy Goal Team at Mill Street Elementary worked with the Department of Education at North Central College to create the Buddy Reading Program. Parents participated in the initial team discussions and worked with the subcommittee as needed.

Planning began with a fall meeting of fourth- and fifth-grade teachers, the reading specialist, the technology integration specialist, the reading instructors from North Central College, and the principal. The technology component proved to be the primary challenge. The Mill Street technology department assisted in arranging Internet access so that the fourth and fifth graders could connect to the North Central College WEBboard. The Buddy Reading Program incurred minimal costs—about $75 for refreshments and $75 for transporting students to North Central College for face-to-face visits. Technology was provided through the school and the college. The college students participated as part of their preservice teaching methodology courses.

Now that the school's Internet access and capacity have been improved, it will be easier to implement communication via WEBboard next year. As a result of the Buddy Reading Program, Mill Street students enhanced their technology and reading comprehension skills while engaging in meaningful dialogue about literature with positive community role models.

ACTIVITY 6: GOAL—IMPROVE STUDENT READING (2002)

Ozzie's Reading Club, a reading incentive program sponsored by the Kane County Cougars minor league baseball team, encouraged Highlands Elementary School students to increase their reading at home. During the eight-week program, approximately 400 students met their identified reading goals, and their families were involved throughout the process.

On January 14th, Ozzie the Cougar, the baseball team's mascot, came to Highlands School to kick off Ozzie's Reading Club. Students attentively listened to stories read by baseball players, the town mayor, parents, and the principal. They got autographs from the players and cheered themselves on as they prepared to boost their reading.

Throughout the eight weeks, students read to "round the bases" (first, second, third, and home plate). Each grade level had a goal in minutes, pages, or books to read during each two-week increment (two weeks equaled one base). The reading was to be done outside of school, either with the family or independently. Parents served as coaches, fans, and umpires for students' reading. At each two-week increment, a parent had to sign a verification form for the student to reach the base. A poster outside of each classroom displayed students' advancement from base to base, and a bulletin board in the school's hallway posted the names of all participating students.

Students who completed the program (made a home run) received an order form good for one free ticket to one of the Ozzie's Reading Club game nights. The form also had spaces where families could order additional tickets for a nominal fee. The tickets included vouchers for a free T-shirt, hot dog, and soda for each participant. The school was very lenient in making the ticket order forms available after the due date to any student who needed to catch up.

The culminating event was a baseball game. All Highlands' families sat in the same general area. Many students attended with both parents and even their grandparents to watch the game and enjoy the activities. Everyone arrived forty-five minutes before the start of the game, and the children marched in a parade led by Ozzie the Cougar. Each participating school was announced, and the children were commended for their hard work in completing the program. They also could have their T-shirts autographed by the mascot and team players. After the game, children went onto the field to run the bases just like the players did during the game. Ozzie's Reading Club energized the school community. Participating for the first time in a school-wide reading incentive program, Highlands School hit a grand slam.

ACTIVITY 7: GOAL—IMPROVE SCHOOL LANDSCAPING (2002)

Since Madison Junior High School opened, nearly 25 years earlier, it had never fully completed the landscaping around the front entrance. Consequently, flooding had been a problem. Skateboarders and rollerbladers also have found the area enticing, resulting in damage to the surrounding walls and concrete. One ATP member mentioned these concerns to her spouse who then created digitally enhanced photographs of the school's front entrance. The pictures showed what could be achieved by painting the concrete walls, adding the name of the school, and making new raised gardens. The team decided to use the pictures as a guide for beautifying the front entrance of the school in time for the twenty-fifth anniversary.

Many people helped bring this plan to fruition. A team of parents and staff raised funds for the project by selling frozen pizzas donated by a local store. The school district grounds department built the raised gardens. A community partner painted the walls and added the name of the school. The school environmental club planted over 500 flower bulbs to bloom in the spring. A parent who owned a garden landscape company donated her time to draw landscape designs. Another parent negotiated with a local nursery, which had formal partnerships with some schools in the district, to supply the plants at a discount and to plant the larger bushes. The school custodians picked up the smaller plants from the nursery. A team of community volunteers planted the shrubs and perennial flowers, working over several days to account for different schedules.

Thanks to this team effort, the school's front entrance was ready for the anniversary celebrations. The school's entrance is now more clearly marked and is an inviting area for visitors. The drainage problems are solved. Skateboarders and rollerbladers seemed to respect the new look of the school, and vandalism has not been a problem.

ACTIVITY 8: GOAL—PROVIDE COMMUNITY SERVICE (2002)

Since 1997, sixth-grade students at Galena Middle School have participated in an ongoing annual quilting project with families, community members, and teachers to provide ill children with beautiful quilts. In the process, students have honed their measuring, geometry, sewing, and social skills while contributing to their community. A Galena Middle School teacher created the project after her own daughter became ill and had received many kindnesses during a long hospital stay. Giving handmade quilts has been a wonderful way to let parents and hospitalized children know that others care about them. The Quilting Project has supported the school improvement goals of academic achievement and family and community involvement. Students have used basic and higher-order thinking skills to solve problems and communicate results.

The Quilting Project usually begins in November with the collection of materials, and then students work on their quilts from December through February. All sixth graders participate in the project. Fathers as well as mothers, aunts, and grandmothers assist the students. Depending on the number of students, teachers, and volunteers participating, an average of twenty to thirty quilts has been constructed per year. Each quilt takes anywhere from ten to twenty-five hours to complete. Thus far, Galena Middle School has donated 147 quilts to area hospitals. Students have followed the listed steps to create their quilts:

Step 1: Students assemble fabric packs, each consisting of a backing fabric and top fabrics cut into four- to five-inch squares).

Step 2: In self-selected groups of three or four, students choose a fabric pack and construct grid patterns for their quilts.

Step 3: Students learn to thread needles, make knots, draw seam allowances, and sew squares and rows together. Parents and family members volunteer to teach sewing classes that focus on reading grids, sewing and pressing seams, running sewing machines, and other skills.

Step 4: Students put the top and backing together and secure it with knots.

School faculty and staff strongly support this project. They donate items and often lend a helping hand to students. Grant money from the state department of education's student services office helps to offset expenses. The greatest challenge faced by the quilting project is the gathering of necessary materials. Quality fabrics are expensive but easier for the students to work with. Parents donate materials, grant money purchases fabrics, and teachers donate the use of sewing machines and other sewing supplies. Depending on the supplies donated, the cash outlay runs between $200 and $600 per year. However, the smiles, tears, hugs, and cuddles received from parents and patients make the quilts priceless.

Students participating in the Quilting Project learn and work with family members, teachers, and peers to do for others rather than themselves. Everyone sees the positive results of the students' work in hospitals where the quilts are displayed until they are given to patients. Some quilts also are shown in the local 4-H Fair held in the county each year. The Quilting Project is evaluated by feedback received from nurses, thank-you notes written by parents of children who received quilts, and teachers' personal visits to the hospitals. The hospitals ask that the students not visit because of the risk of germs. As an alternative, pictures capture the deliveries and students read the thank-you notes and other comments kept in a class scrapbook. To enhance the Quilting Project, the teacher has created a Web page to help students learn more about quilting, its history, and its connections with math.

ACTIVITY 9: GOAL—IMPROVE STUDENT ORAL AND WRITTEN COMMUNICATION (2004)

Imagine how different life would be without pizza. McKinley Elementary School students got a chance to hear many such tales through an intergenerational writing project. McKinley's partnership team invited their community's Retired Senior Volunteer Program (RSVP) to school for a day of sharing life stories. Students interviewed the visitors with questions they prepared ahead of time, and each of the seniors gave detailed, memorable answers. Afterwards, students wrote about the stories they heard and sent thank-you notes to the senior volunteers.

The idea for the Intergenerational Writing Project originated during one of McKinley's ATP meetings. Team members brainstormed different partnership ideas that could support student writing. The Intergenerational Writing Project was selected, since it would appeal to students as well as achieve academic goals. To gain support for the idea, team members publicized the project through their school's newsletter. Members also determined the number of senior volunteers needed in each classroom and the length of the interviews. Then the team collaborated with teachers to decide how the interview process would work and what students would do with the senior's information.

The partnership team worked with the coordinator of RSVP and teachers to set up a time for the seniors to visit participating classrooms. On the day of the interviews, students escorted the senior volunteers to their assigned classrooms. In addition to enjoying an afternoon together, students and seniors gained other benefits from the Intergenerational Writing Project. Seniors gave intriguing answers to the students' questions about life before they were born. One student was sorry that seniors never had video games, and another couldn't understand how they survived childhood without pizza! Academically, students improved their literacy skills by writing stories and thank-you notes. The RSVP visit was the talk of the school for days to come.

McKinley Elementary School encouraged other schools to take full advantage of senior volunteer groups in their community, for they are a valuable resource in building partnerships and improving student success.

ACTIVITY 10: GOAL—IMPROVE FACILITIES FOR STUDENTS WITH DISABILITIES (2004)

The William S. Baer School serves students with disabilities from ages 3 to 21 and students without disabilities from ages 3 to 5. Therapists have been working for years with Baer students on self-help and toileting skills. However, the school's toilets and sinks were fashioned for adults with disabilities and had not been renovated since the early 1980s. Children were unable to use the facilities independently. Baer School's Partnership Board set out to renovate the facilities so that all students could reach the school goal of preparing for independent living.

Approximately twenty members composed the Partnership Board, including educators, businessmen, teachers, politicians, and parents. The board was founded to provide funds and materials to assist staff members in improving the quality of life for students. The Partnership Board decided to plan for the bathroom renovations. Board members met with parents, teachers, and students to explain the need for renovated bathrooms and ask for suggestions.

After taking suggestions from therapists, teachers, and parents, the Board agreed to sponsor a 5K race to raise $175,000, the estimated cost to renovate four bathrooms. Board members recruited sponsors, ordered T-shirts, and secured donations of bottled water. Students participated as cheerleaders at the finish line.

Renovation of the four bathrooms has made them more accessible; met the needs of students, teachers, and therapists; and allowed students to practice their self-help skills. Through practice, many more students are now able to take care of their personal needs independently. Parents, staff, and students are delighted with the gains in independence. As Baer School's principal described, "I truly believe this project has increased the quality of life for these students."

ACTIVITY 11: GOAL—IMPROVE STUDENT SCIENCE SKILLS (2000)

Picture this: It's a cold rainy January day, and a group of students and parents are hiking a three-mile stretch. It's a warm April day, and the same group is saying, "Let's move that topsoil!" "Hold that wheelbarrow!" These fourth-grade students and parents are enjoying a classroom without walls.

The state's bureau of parks envisioned local schools planning, planting, and maintaining gardens along a local nature trail. A group of fourth graders at Bentalou Elementary School was selected as one of three local classes to participate in the project.

The students learned about scientific phenomena as they watched plants grow, and they enriched their vocabularies with terms like *transplant*, *germinate*, and *pollinate*. Under the direction of the state's coordinator of environmental education, participating students engaged in classroom sessions in which they learned how landscaping techniques benefit the bay watershed. The coordinator also directed hiking trips in which the students surveyed the garden, marked off the boundaries, chose native plants, prepared the ground for planting, and watered the garden.

The project's curriculum had direct links to the science, social studies, reading, and math classes. Activities related to the state's proficiency exam also were incorporated. The project stimulated and motivated these fourth graders and their parents to respect and preserve nature, the Gwynns Falls Trail, and the rivers and streams in the area.

ACTIVITY 12: GOAL—PROVIDE AFTERSCHOOL ACTIVITIES FOR MIDDLE SCHOOL STUDENTS (2000)

Beginning in 1997 and continuing to the time of this writing, the Involvement Coordinators at Chaska Middle School have partnered with community agencies to develop an exciting opportunity to keep young adolescents out of trouble by engaging them in afterschool activities. Local recreation programs had been struggling with successful ways to get teens involved in activities other than school sports. A survey of the school's sixth through ninth graders revealed that teens were interested in, but faced obstacles to, participation in afterschool programs. Based on survey results, a program was designed that incorporated professional staff expertise; nonduplication of services between agencies; social opportunities for young teens; and a safe, positive environment that families could embrace. One year later, Club Mid began.

Club Mid serves as an alternative to traditional competitive athletics by offering to middle school students three different series of clubs during the school year. Using mainly school facilities, each four- to eight-week-long club meets weekly for one to two hours after school. Club themes include computers, board games, cooking, drama, snowboarding, weightlifting, and other activities. Teachers or community volunteers with an interest in the activity lead the clubs.

A planning team of representatives from the school and local service agencies meets prior to each new quarter to review the previous club series, brainstorm ideas, and choose the clubs to implement next. One member of the team compiles the details into a flyer that is then promoted through school communications, local newspapers, the team's member agencies, and libraries.

The clubs generally serve sixth- and seventh-grade students, although students up to the ninth grade are encouraged to participate. Each series has about 150 students registered. Clubs are limited to ten to thirty students led by one adult. Registration fees, about $10–$30, help to cover the costs of supplies and leadership hours. Leaders are paid on the same scale as sport coaches. Club Mid began with some seed money designated from school donations and funds, but it is now a self-supporting program.

There are five cities in the school district with numerous service agencies that target the teen population. The initial challenge was to combine the talents and resources of these many professionals in order to meet the adolescents' needs. By working collaboratively with the school, the agencies were able to access their teen market. Team members found they could accomplish a common goal by sharing responsibilities based on individual strengths. A liaison from the school has been a critical link to ensuring partner relationships.

Program results have been very positive. Students have looked forward to their social interactions with friends and have discovered adults can be fun people (rather than always the authority!). With improved promotion efforts, parents have begun to call ahead to find out what was being offered so they could plan for the upcoming season. Planning team members have continued to support the program with staff time. Other programs in the district have begun to use the Club Mid structure as a model. The best measure of the program's success has come from the written evaluations completed by students at the close of every season. We know we have reached the kids when we read, "Club Mid is awesome."

SUMMARY

These activities demonstrate the variety of goals that can be addressed through community partnerships. They also show that partnerships can be designed to achieve both academic and nonacademic goals. A quilting project, for example, can achieve service learning, math, and parental involvement goals, and in so doing, extend and enrich students' learning experience. A career week can introduce students to new professions as well as provide research and writing opportunities. The following chapter provides tools to conduct a professional development workshop on community partnerships to prepare educational leaders to conduct this important work.

8 Preparing Educational Leaders for Community Partnerships

A Workshop Agenda

Well-designed and implemented community partnerships can help any school maximize its effectiveness for students. Professional development on the topic helps to ensure that school leaders have the capacity to conduct meaningful community partnerships to achieve school goals. This chapter describes an approximately two-and-one-half-hour workshop that can be conducted with one or more teams responsible for coordinating and implementing school-based community partnerships.

First, the agenda is presented. Then, each section of the workshop is discussed in detail. Accompanying handouts also are included that can be copied for overhead projectors or reproduced for PowerPoint presentations. The agenda is designed to provide participants with (a) essential information on community partnerships, (b) opportunities to practice key aspects of developing and planning community partnerships, and (c) time to reflect on the implementation of such partnerships at their school sites.

While this workshop is usually conducted with at least twenty participants, it can be modified for larger or smaller groups. Where applicable,

I describe how such modifications can be made. Facilitators conducting this workshop—whether school or district administrators or teacher-leaders—also are encouraged to extend or modify the workshop by including activities taken from other chapters in the book.

BUILDING COMMUNITY PARTNERSHIPS AGENDA*

Overview

- Introduction (10–15 minutes)
- Identifying potential community partners and foci for partnerships (15 minutes)
- Developing goal-focused community partnerships (small group activity, 30 minutes)
- Break (10–15 minutes)
- Overcoming obstacles to community partnerships (whole group and paired activity, 30 minutes)
- Attracting community partners (20 minutes)
- Taking action (10 minutes)
- Questions and answers and evaluation (10 minutes)

Materials and Equipment Needed

1. Overhead projector or LCD projector, screen, and laptop

2. Flipchart and markers

3. Notepads for participants' notes

4. Notebooks for workshop materials

Introduction

Workshop facilitators should take this opportunity to introduce themselves to their groups and to describe their interest in and experience with the topic. Participants also should have the opportunity to introduce themselves, describing their professional positions as well as interest in and experience with community partnerships. If time permits, participants might also be

---

*This workshop agenda should be reformatted to include date and exact times as determined by the workshop facilitator.

given the opportunity to share, either with the entire group or with one or two other individuals, one exemplary community partnership they have either observed or helped to implement. After introductions, the facilitator can transition to the next section by reviewing the importance of community partnerships (see Handout 8.1, Why Not Schools Alone; all the handouts mentioned can be found in sequence at the end of the chapter. Also review Chapters 1 and 2).

Identifying Potential Community Partners and Foci for Partnerships

After introductions, the facilitator should introduce the list of potential community partners. Many school-based administrators and leaders think narrowly about community partners, focusing primarily on businesses. Those in areas with few small or large businesses are often convinced that they cannot successfully incorporate community partnerships in their school improvement efforts. By introducing the variety of community partners listed in Handout 8.2 (Community Partners), workshop facilitators can broaden participants' definition of *community*.

Furthermore, participants should be helped to understand that community partnerships can be designed to achieve goals for students, families, schools, and communities. This topic is discussed in detail in Chapter 1 and shown in Handout 8.3 (Partnership Activity Foci). Last, facilitators should use Handout 8.4 (Community Partnerships: Range of Complexity) to illustrate the range of complexity into which community partnerships can fall. Participants should be helped to recognize differences between simple and complex partnerships. Participants also should be guided in understanding that schools with little experience with partnerships should begin with more simple connections, and as their capacity grows, they should incorporate more complex partnerships into their school improvement efforts. At the end of the section, facilitators should encourage participants to share experiences and ask questions. For example, the facilitator might ask, "Does anyone have an example of a complex partnership that was successfully implemented at your school?" Follow-up questions might include, "What was the most challenging aspect of the activity?" "What were the results?"

Developing Goal-Focused Community Partnerships

This section should begin with a discussion of the importance of linking partnerships to meaningful goals. (Facilitators should review Chapters 1 and 4 prior to the workshop.) To give participants experience in developing goal-focused partnerships with different foci, partners, and levels of complexity, the facilitator should guide participants in completing the exercise described in Handout 8.5 (Small-group Activity). This exercise is designed to model the process that partnership teams should engage in at their school sites.

For small groups, have participants work individually. For larger groups, divide participants into teams to complete the exercise. While participants are working, the facilitator should move from group to group to ensure that participants are attending to both the goals and the complexity. At the end of the exercise, the facilitator should give participants the opportunity to share their activities.

Break

Participants should be given a ten-minute break.

Overcoming Obstacles to Community Partnerships

To prepare for this section, the facilitator should first review the discussion of obstacles in Chapter 1 and the vignette described in Chapter 4. The facilitator should begin this section by asking participants to describe obstacles that they have faced or anticipate facing when developing community partnerships. Responses can be written on an overhead or on a flip board. After about five (5) obstacles have been identified, the facilitator should give participants five minutes to discuss in pairs potential ways to address an assigned obstacle from the list generated. After the paired sharing, the facilitator should ask participants to share their suggestions with the entire group (about 10–15 minutes) and write these on the flip chart. Finally, the facilitator should use Handout 8.6 (Overcoming Obstacles to Community Partnerships) to identify additional solutions to common obstacles to partnerships, such as lack of community partners, lack of support for community partnerships, and lack of continuity in community partnerships. When discussing Solution 5 in Handout 8.6, the facilitator should introduce the annual catalog of community partners (Handout 8.7).

Attracting Community Partners

In this section, the facilitator should focus on four major factors identified by community partners as important to their engagement (see Handout 8.8, What Attracts Community Partners to a School):

1. *Schools' commitment to learning.* Facilitators should emphasize that schools do not have to be the best in their district or state but must show that they are functional and focused on systematically improving student outcomes.

2. *Principal support*. Facilitators should emphasize that principals are not expected to manage every aspect of a community partnership; however, principal support and enthusiasm for partnerships are important to attract and maintain effective partnerships, as discussed in Handout 8.9 (What Principals Can Do . . .).

3. *A welcoming climate*. Facilitators should emphasize that community partners are more likely to engage in partnerships with schools that are welcoming.

4. *Clear communication*. Facilitators should emphasize that schools must communicate their goals clearly to community partners and also engage in two-way communication to identify mutually acceptable ways in which community partners can assist in achieving them.

Sample letters in Resource B should be introduced as tools to support school-community communication. Once information is reviewed, facilitators should be prepared to field questions about each of these elements. To prepare for this section, facilitators should review Chapters 3 through 7.

Taking Action

The facilitator should encourage participants to reflect on what they have learned by completing the questions shown in Handout 8.10 (Taking Action), either individually or in pairs. If time permits, have participants share their next steps with the whole group.

Questions and Answers and Evaluation

The facilitator should allot time for final questions and comments. Participants should also be given the opportunity to complete the evaluation shown in Handout 8.11 (Workshop on Community Partnerships).

SUMMARY

This workshop will provide participants with the basic information needed to begin to develop meaningful, goal-focused partnerships. Facilitators should feel free to modify the workshop as needed to address the specific needs and concerns of their audiences. Activities in Resource A, for example, might be used to provide participants with more opportunities to discuss the identification of community partners (Activity 1), improving existing community partnerships (Activities 2 and 3), and garnering principal support for community partnerships (Activity 4). Facilitators also can photocopy chapters that they believe will further enhance participants' understanding and preparation. Chapter 1 provides a broad overview of key concepts, Chapter 4 provides suggestions for getting started in low-readiness schools, and Chapter 7 provides several examples of promising community partnership practices. These or other chapters, as well as relevant handouts, should be included in a binder and given to participants to use as reference material once the workshop is completed.

HANDOUT 8.1

WHY NOT SCHOOLS ALONE:

Facts about school, family, and community partnerships and students' success

- Family and community engagement in schools has been consistently linked to higher student achievement and graduation rates as well as improved student behavior and school attendance.

- High-achieving students of all ages and backgrounds spend at least nine hours of out-of-school time per week in activities such as reading, writing, and study guided by adults. In contrast, low-achieving students spend more time on unstructured activities, like hanging out, talking on the phone, playing video games, and watching television.

- Parent and community engagement in schools can lead to more welcoming, better resourced, and higher-functioning schools.

HANDOUT 8.2

COMMUNITY PARTNERS

Types of Community Partners	For example . . .
Business/Corporations	Local businesses, national corporations and franchises
Universities and Educational Institutions	Colleges, universities, high schools, and other educational institutions
Health Care Organizations	Hospitals, health care centers, mental health facilities, health departments, health foundations and associations
Government and Military Agencies	Fire departments, police departments, chambers of commerce, city councils, other local and state government agencies and departments
National Service and Volunteer Organizations	Rotary Club, Lions Club, Kiwanis Club, VISTA, Concerned Black Men, Inc., Shriners, Boy and Girl Scouts, YWCA, United Way, AmeriCorps, Urban League
Faith Organizations	Churches, mosques, synagogues, other religious organizations and charities
Senior Citizens Organizations	Nursing homes, senior volunteer and service organizations
Cultural and Recreational Institutions	Zoos, museums, libraries, recreational centers
Media Organizations	Local newspapers, radio stations, cable networks
Sports Franchises and Associations	Minor and major league sports teams, NBA, NCAA
Other Community Organizations	Fraternities, sororities; foundations, neighborhood associations; political, alumni, and local service organizations
Community Individuals	Individual volunteers from the surrounding school community

HANDOUT 8.3

PARTNERSHIP ACTIVITY FOCI

● Student-centered

(Student awards, student incentives, scholarships, student trips, tutors, mentors, job shadowing, and other services and products for students)

● Family-centered

(Parent workshops, family fun nights, GED and other adult education classes, parent incentives and rewards, counseling and other forms of assistance, etc.)

● School-centered

(Equipment and materials, beautification and repair, teacher incentives and awards, funds for school events and programs, office and classroom assistance, etc.)

● Community-centered

(Community beautification, student exhibits and performances, charity and other outreach, etc.)

HANDOUT 8.4

COMMUNITY PARTNERSHIPS:
RANGE OF COMPLEXITY

SIMPLE PARTNERSHIPS

(e.g., incentives for school activities; donation of school materials/supplies)

COMPLEX PARTNERSHIPS

(e.g., full-service schools; professional development schools)

- Short term

- Unidirectional exchange

- Low level of interaction

- Limited planning

- Long term

- Bi- or multidirectional exchange

- High level of interaction

- Extensive planning and coordination

HANDOUT 8.5

SMALL-GROUP ACTIVITY

Work individually or in a small group to write a brief description of a simple or complex partnership activity that can be conducted with the assigned partner to achieve the assigned goal.

Group 1

School goal—higher reading scores for Grades 1–3
Local library—simple

Group 2

School goal—higher student attendance for Grades 6–8
Local hospital—complex

Group 3

School goal—higher science scores on state proficiency test for high school students
Local college or university—complex

Group 4

School goal—improved parent involvement for an elementary school (Grades 1–5)
Local supermarket—simple

Group 5

School goal—higher mathematics scores for Grade 5
Local newspaper—complex

HANDOUT 8.6

OVERCOMING OBSTACLES
TO COMMUNITY PARTNERSHIPS

1. Cast a wide net when fishing for community partners to increase the potential pool.

2. Gather pertinent information on state, district, and school guidelines before entering into partnerships, to avoid prohibited interactions.

3. Lay a firm foundation by allowing sufficient time for planning, implementing, and evaluating partnership activities, to increase the likelihood of successful outcomes and broader support.

4. Establish partnerships that will help to achieve specified goals (learn when and how to say "yes" and "no") to ensure progress toward a vision of excellence.

5. Maintain a record of community partners and activities to support program planning and encourage continuity.

6. Communicate at least twice annually (beginning and end of school year) with community partners to provide an update on goals and progress and to encourage continued involvement.

HANDOUT 8.7

ANNUAL CATALOG
OF COMMUNITY PARTNERS

School Name: _____

Community Partnerships Coordinator: _____

School Year: _____

COMMUNITY PARTNER	PARTNERSHIP ACTIVITY*
Name Address Contact Information	

Name
Address
Contact Information

_____

Name
Address
Contact Information

_____

Name
Address
Contact Information

_____

Name
Address
Contact Information

_____

*Indicate whether new or ongoing activity

HANDOUT 8.8

WHAT ATTRACTS COMMUNITY PARTNERS TO A SCHOOL

- School's commitment to learning

- Principal's support and enthusiasm

- A welcoming school climate

- Clear communication and flexibility about the level and kind of community involvement

HANDOUT 8.9

WHAT PRINCIPALS CAN DO TO PROMOTE EFFECTIVE COMMUNITY PARTNERSHIPS

- Maintain a school environment where teachers and parents are focused on students' academic success

- Model for faculty and staff a genuine openness to community involvement, and establish an expectation for partnerships

- Network with individuals in the community to inform them of the school's needs and goals

- Play an active and supportive role on the school's Action Team for Partnerships

- Assist other school personnel in developing leadership for family and community involvement

HANDOUT 8.10

TAKING ACTION: YOUR NEXT STEPS FOR IMPROVING COMMUNITY PARTNERSHIPS FOR STUDENT SUCCESS

1. What are three important things that you learned about school-community partnerships in this session?

2. How will you act on this information at your school?

HANDOUT 8.11

WORKSHOP ON COMMUNITY PARTNERSHIPS

Date:

Please circle how much you agree or disagree with each statement.

	Strongly Disagree (SD)	Disagree (D)	Agree (A)	Strongly Agree (SA)
Structure				
The goals of this workshop were clear.	SD	D	A	SA
The goals of this workshop were met.	SD	D	A	SA
Time was used well.	SD	D	A	SA
Content				
I gained many ideas that will help me or my school.	SD	D	A	SA
I feel better prepared to work with communities to achieve important goals for students' learning.	SD	D	A	SA
There were opportunities to share ideas with others.	SD	D	A	SA
Overall, this workshop was worthwhile.	SD	D	A	SA

Other comments or ideas on the workshop:

_____

_____

_____

_____

What assistance or follow-up would you like?

_____

_____

_____

_____

Thank you for your feedback!

9 Concluding Thoughts

Community partnerships alone cannot ensure a school's effectiveness. However, such partnerships are an important strategy for creating inclusive schools that possess the human and material resources needed to meet the educational needs of increasingly diverse student populations. This book has provided a broad overview of the topic. Its primary goal has been to increase the capacity of educational leaders to incorporate community partnerships in their school improvement efforts. For readers who would like to further explore key aspects of school, family, and community partnerships, I recommend the following resources and wish you much success in your school improvement efforts.

Henderson, A., & Mapp, K. (2002). *A new wave of evidence: The impact of school, family, and community connections on student achievement*. Austin, TX: Southwest Educational Development Laboratory.

> This research report describes and synthesizes fifty-one recent research studies about the impact of family and community involvement on student achievement and related outcomes and strategies to improve school, family, and community connections. It is one of the most comprehensive reviews of the research literature on school partnerships currently available. It concludes with useful recommendations for practice. It is well written and organized and an indispensable resource for researchers and practitioners in the field. It is available online at www.sedl.org/connections/resources/evidence.pdf.

Epstein, J. L., Sanders, M. G., Salinas, K., Simon, B., VanVoorhis, F., & Jansorn, N. (2002). *School, family and community partnerships: Your handbook for action* (2nd ed**.**)*.* Thousand Oaks, CA: Corwin.

> This book focuses specifically on community involvement in schools and provides a research-based approach to incorporating both families and communities in students' learning and schools' improvement efforts. Specifically, it

presents a framework of six types of involvement to broaden practitioners' understanding of how families and communities influence students' success. It also guides educational leaders in developing school-based ATPs and provides important planning, programmatic, and evaluation tools. It is an essential resource for partnership program development and maintenance.

Dryfoos, J., & Maguire, S. (2002). *Inside full-service community schools.* Thousand Oaks, CA: Corwin.

Some of the most complex of community partnerships are full-service schools. Joy Dryfoos, a national policy analyst, and Sue Maguire, a school principal, provide an insightful account of how urban, rural, and suburban schools can effectively integrate health services, community-based programs, and academics to support the learning needs of diverse students. The book guides policymakers and practitioners in the process of developing full-service schools—from getting started and finding funding to overcoming obstacles to implementation and sustainability. It is a useful and timely addition to the current literature on school-community connections.

Rubin, H. (2002). *Collaborative leadership: Developing effective partnerships in communities and schools.* Thousands Oaks, CA: Corwin.

For educators who seek to lead partnerships in schools, districts, or states and who would like to refresh their collaborative leadership skills, Hank Rubin's book will be useful. Of particular note are Rubin's discussions of the contexts and purposes of collaboration. He reminds us of when and why collaboration is important, especially in educational contexts. His discussion of the seven essential characteristics of effective collaborative leaders also is useful. Whether novices or experienced educational leaders, readers will be exposed to important tools of the craft.

Resource A

Sample Activities

Activity 1
Locating Community Partners

If you are just beginning to develop community partnerships at your school or would like to reach new community partners, try this four-step process:

1. EXPLORE the area within a one-mile radius of your school.

   Depending on the density of the area around your school, you may extend the exploration to up to a five-mile radius. However, begin in your own back yard. These potential partners are easy to reach. Also, they may have a vested interest in working with your school population (e.g., they may be alumni of your school and wish to contribute, they may be service agencies whose target population overlaps with your school population, or they might be businesses interested in expanding their clientele).

2. IDENTIFY the names and addresses of businesses, organizations, and agencies with whom you might partner.

   Based on your exploration and possible partners identified in Table 1.2, develop your list of potential partners. Do not overlook other schools with which you might want to establish an exchange (e.g., a local high school might provide childcare for an elementary school during parent-teacher conferences). Also consider residents of the community who may want to help during a school clean-up day or participate in a community garden project.

3. THINK about the school improvement goals that these partners might help you to achieve.

   As discussed briefly in Chapter 1, goal-oriented community partnerships help schools achieve visions of excellence. Think about your school goals and be able to articulate them clearly before you approach a potential partner.

4. CONTACT the partners that you have identified as most promising.

   By starting in your backyard, you can meet with potential partners face to face. Teams can divide the task so that each member is responsible for contacting one potential partner, or two members might be responsible for contacting three potential partners each, and so on. Face-to-face contacts are more personal and do not require potential community partners to read and respond to a formal letter or survey, which can be time consuming. School representatives should follow up these initial contacts with letters that either confirm verbal agreements or establish the potential for further communication and future partnerships. Examples of two types of community partnership letters are found in Resource B.

Activity 2
Improving the Partnership Process

Think of your school's most and least effective community partnerships. Compare them using the following questions:

1. How was the partnership initiated?

2. Were the goals of the partnership clear?

3. Did the school and the community partner have equal input into the development of the collaboration?

4. Who were the school representatives responsible for overseeing development of the community partnerships?

5. What modes of communication were used to maintain contact? What was the frequency of communication?

Most Effective Community Partnership	Least Effective Community Partnership
1.	1.
2.	2.
3.	3.
4.	4.
5.	5.

If your comparison generates different responses to one or more of these questions, consider applying the processes used in the most effective partnership to future community collaborations.

Activity 3
Improving Community Partnership Quality

Before planning your community partnerships for the upcoming school year, use the following quality scale to rate your school's current community partnerships.

1. Not yet started

2. Beginning, with only a few simple partnerships

3. Well developed, with several partnerships that range in complexity but that are not clearly aligned with school improvement goals

4. Well developed, with several partnerships that range in complexity and are clearly aligned with school improvement goals but have a limited focus (e.g., focused primarily on students)

5. Well developed, with a combination of partnerships that range in complexity, are clearly aligned with school improvement goals, and are broadly focused on parents, students, the school, *and* the community

Based on your rating and information gleaned from this book, identify three action steps that your school can take to achieve higher quality partnerships.

Action Step 1:

Action Step 2:

Action Step 3:

Activity 4
Garnering Principal Support for Partnerships

As discussed, principal support is *critical* for successful school-community partnerships. However, many schools report lack of principal support as a major obstacle to partnerships. If your school is having difficulty garnering needed principal support for community partnerships, consider the following strategies. Which might help? What other ways might your school encourage the principal to support community outreach efforts?

A. *Develop a plan:* Clearly outline how the community partnerships that you propose can help to achieve one or more important school goals. Also clearly and realistically outline what school resources will be needed to ensure the partnership's success.

B. *Identify a bridge:* Solicit the support of a person or committee (e.g., school improvement or site-based management team, PTA or PTO) in your school that has credibility with the principal. Encourage the credible party to present the idea to the principal and to act as co-coordinator of the collaborative project.

C. *Find external support:* Explore local or national organizations, such as the National Network of Partnership Schools (www.partnershipschools.org), to gain research-based information, guidelines, and support for school, family, and community partnerships.

Resource B

Sample Letters

Sample Letter 1
Partnership Communication

Sample Letter 1 might be used before or after a face-to-face meeting or telephone call with an interested community partner. I provide two versions of the letter. The first, Letter 1A, should be used if a specific partnership has been agreed on. Letter 1B should be used if communication has occurred but a firm agreement to partner has not been reached.

Letter 1A

School Letterhead

Date

Dear (name of contact person):

I enjoyed speaking with you on (day and date of meeting or telephone conversation.). Thank you for taking the time to discuss our school's current goals. Your decision to (describe partnership, including any agreed upon dates and times) is sincerely appreciated.

If you need to contact me for any reason, please do not hesitate to do so at (e-mail address, telephone number, or both). The partnership team (or include the name of the team) at (name of school) is excited to work with you to support our students' learning and success.

Sincerely,

(Name, position)

Letter 1B

School Letterhead

Date

Dear (name of contact person):

I enjoyed speaking with you on (day and date of meeting or telephone conversation). Thank you for taking the time to discuss our school's current goals. I look forward to speaking with you again (if date and time has been determined, include here) as we further explore partnership possibilities.

If you need to contact me for any reason, please do not hesitate to do so at (e-mail address, telephone number, or both). On behalf of the partnership team at (name of school), I hope that we have the opportunity to work together to support students' learning and school success.

Sincerely,

(Name, position)

Sample Letter 2
Partnership Activity Follow-Up

This letter might be used after the completion of a partnership activity or at the end of a school year to keep community partners informed of school progress.

School Letterhead

Date

Dear (name of contact person):

(Name of school) sincerely enjoyed partnering with you this academic year. It has been an exciting and successful year. (Describe one area of significant progress, for example, "Of note, our students' attendance rate increased from 93% to 95%.")

Your generosity has made a significant difference at (name of school). As a result of (describe specific partnership contribution.), (describe results for targeted population if available; if such information is not available, skip to final sentence). We hope to partner with you again next year as our school continues to progress toward the highest standards of educational excellence.

Yours truly,

(Name, position of school contact)   (Name of principal, if different from
                                                           school contact)

Endnotes

1. I also use the terms *school-community partnerships* and *school-community collaboration* to account for such connections. For the purposes of this book, I use these terms interchangeably and not to denote differences in the intensity or complexity of the connections.

2. For an extended discussion, see Nettles's (1991) article.

3. The research on which this book is based was supported by grants from several funding sources, including the Spencer Foundation, The Dewitt-Wallace Foundation, and the U.S. Department of Education, Office of Educational Research and Improvement, and Institute of Education Sciences. The opinions expressed are the author's and do not necessarily represent the positions or policies of the funding agencies.

4. For more information on NNPS, visit the organization's Web site at www .partnershipschools.org.

5. Of the 443 schools in the sample, about one third were located in large cities (34%), over one quarter were located in suburban areas (27%); 20% were located in small cities, and about 19% were located in rural areas. The majority (70%) was elementary schools serving only students from prekindergarten to Grade 6; 14% were middle schools that include only students from Grades 4 through 9; 7% were high schools with students between Grades 9 and 12; and 9% were schools that serve students from a range of grade levels. Sixty-five percent of the schools in the sample receive some Title 1 funds, and 43% were schoolwide Title 1 programs. One third of the schools reported that their students' families spoke between two and five languages other than English. For a full description of the study, see Sanders (2001).

6. While the model in this chapter was derived from over five years of research in the field, I draw heavily from case studies conducted during 2000–2003 to illustrate the significance of the components described. The research was conducted at an urban elementary school (see Sanders & Harvey, 2002) and three high schools—one urban, one suburban, and one rural (see Sanders & Lewis, in press-a). The case schools were selected based on the length and quality of their community partnerships. Names have been changed to protect anonymity and confidentiality. See the references mentioned for more information on the methods used in these studies.

7. Pseudonyms are used to ensure participants' anonymity and confidentiality.

8. For a discussion of the evolution of a team approach to partnership program development, see Sanders and Epstein (2000).

9. *Janet* is a pseudonym for a young teacher that I had the opportunity to work closely with on a leadership project for school, family, and community partnerships.

Through our close contact over two years, I witnessed firsthand how a teacher-leader can build a school's capacity for successful community partnerships.

10. To read more about these high schools, see Sanders and Lewis (in press-a, in press-b).

11. To review more activities submitted by NNPS schools, visit the Web site at www. partnershipschools.org

References

Abell, S. (2000). From professor to colleague: Creating a professional identity as collaborator in elementary science. *Journal of Research in Science Teaching, 37*(6), 548–562.

Alvarado, V. (1997). *Service-learning, an effective teaching strategy for Texas middle schools.* Washington, DC: Office of Educational Research and Improvement.

Amato, C. (1996). Freedom elementary school and its community: An approach to school-linked service integration. *Remedial and Special Education, 17*(5), 303–309.

American Jewish Congress, Christian Legal Society, & First Amendment Center, Vanderbilt University. (1999). *Public schools and religious communities: A First Amendment guide.* Annandale, VA: Author.

Ascher, C. (1988). *Urban school-community alliances.* New York: ERIC Clearinghouse on Urban Education. (ERIC Document Reproduction Service No. ED306339)

Badiali, B., Flora, R., Johnson, I., & Shiveley, J. (2000). Beyond collaboration: Accounts of partnership from the Institute for Educational Renewal based at Miami University. *Peabody Journal of Education, 75*(3), 145–160.

Bauch, P. (2001). School-community partnerships in rural schools: Leadership, renewal, and a sense of place. *Peabody Journal of Education, 76*(2), 204–221.

Behrman, R. (Ed). (1992, Spring). School linked services. *Future of Children, 2,* 6–18.

Benson, P. (1996). Beyond the "village" rhetoric: What makes a healthy community for children and adolescents? *Assets Magazine, 1*(1), 3–4.

Benton, J., Zath, R., & Hensley, F. (1996). Negotiating school-university partnerships: Participants' voices in co-reform. *Urban Review, 28,* 257–78.

Bermudez, A., & Padron, Y. (1988). University-school collaboration that increases minority parent involvement. *Educational Horizons, 66*(2), 83–86.

Beyerbach, B. A., Weber, S., Swift, J. N., & Gooding, C. T. (1996). A school/business/university partnership for professional development. *School Community Journal, 6*(1), 101–112.

Borthwick, A. (1995, April). *School-university community collaboration: Establishing and maintaining partnerships for school improvement.* Paper presented at the meeting of the American Educational Research Association, San Francisco, CA.

Bruner, C. (1991). *Thinking collaboratively: Ten questions and answers to help policy makers improve children's services.* Washington, DC: Education and Human Services Consortium.

Bucy, H. (1990). *School-community-business partnerships: Building foundations for dropout prevention.* Clemson, SC: National Dropout Prevention Center.

Burch, P., & Palanki, A. (1995). *From clients to partners: Four case studies of collaboration and family involvement in the development of school-linked services* (Report 29). Baltimore, MD: Johns Hopkins University, Center on Families, Communities, Schools, & Children's Learning.

Burstein, N., Kretschmer, D., Smith, C., & Gudoski, P. (1999). Redesigning teacher education as a shared responsibility of schools and universities. *Journal of Teacher Education, 50*(2), 106–118.

Carr, A. (1997). Leadership and community participation: Four case studies. *Journal of Curriculum and Supervision, 12,* 152–168.

Cohen, D. (1991, November 13). Recession forces states to turn budget ax on programs to support children, families. *Education Week, 1,* 17.

Coleman, J. (1987). Families and schools. *Educational Researcher, 16*(6), 32–38.

Coleman, J. (1988). Social capital and schools. *Education Digest, 53,* 6–9.

Combs, L., & Bailey, G. (1992). Exemplary school-community partnerships: Successful programs. *Rural Educator, 13*(3), 8–13.

Crowson, R. L., & Boyd, W. (1993). Coordinated services for children: Designing arks for storms and seas unknown. *American Journal of Education, 101,* 140–179.

Cushing, E., & Kohl, E. (1997). *Allies for education—Community involvement in school change: A two-year exploration.* San Francisco: San Francisco School Volunteers & Hewlett Foundation.

Darling-Hammond, L. (1994). *Professional development schools: Schools for developing a profession.* New York: Teachers College Press.

Dolan, L. (1992, March). *Models for integrating human services into the schools* (Report No. 30). Baltimore: Johns Hopkins University, Center for Social Organization of Schools.

Dryfoos, J. (1994). *Full-service schools: A revolution in health and social services for children, youth and families.* San Francisco: Jossey-Bass.

Dryfoos, J. (1998). The rise of the full-service community school. *High School Magazine, 6*(2), 38–42.

Dryfoos, J. (2002). Full-service community schools: Creating new institutions. *Phi Delta Kappan, 83*(5), 393–399.

Dryfoos, J. (2003). A community school in action. *Reclaiming Children and Youth, 11*(4), 203–205.

Dryfoos, J., & Maguire, S. (2002). *Inside full-service community schools.* Thousand Oaks, CA: Corwin.

Ebert, C. (1997). A new institution: The emerging educational community in an effective professional development school. *Action in Teacher Education, 19*(2), 55–62.

Engeln, J. (2003). Guiding school/business partnerships. *Education Digest, 68*(7), 36–40.

Epstein, J. L. (1991, January). Paths to partnership: What we can learn from federal, state, district and school initiatives. *Phi Delta Kappan, 72*(5), 344–349.

Epstein, J. L. (1995). School/family/community partnerships: Caring for the children we share. *Phi Delta Kappan, 76*(9), 701–712.

Epstein, J. L., Sanders, M. G., Salinas, K., Simon, B., VanVoorhis, F., & Jansorn, N. (2002). *School, family and community partnerships: Your handbook for action* (2nd ed.). Thousand Oaks, CA: Corwin.

Eyler, J., Lynch, C., & Gray, C. (1997, March). *Service learning and the development of reflective judgment.* Paper presented at the annual meeting of the American Educational Research Association, Chicago.

Families and Work Institute. (1995). *Employers, families and education: Promoting family involvement in learning.* Washington, DC: U.S. Department of Education.

Fitzgerald, J. (1997). Linking school-to-work programs to community economic development in urban schools. *Urban Education, 32*(4), 489–511.

Floyd, L. (1998). Joining hands: A parent involvement program. *Urban Education, 33*, 123–135.

Gallagher, R., Knowlton, E., Mahlios, M., & Kleinhammer-Tramill, J. (1997). *Trends in integrated service delivery: Implications for the art and science of collaboration.* Paper presented at the Annual Convention of the Council for Exceptional Children, Salt Lake City, UT.

Gardner, R., III, Cartledge, G., Seidl, B., Woolsey, M., Schley, G., & Utley, C. (2001). Mt. Olivet After-School Program: Peer-mediated interventions for at-risk students. *Remedial and Special Education, 22*(1), 22–23.

Gray, B. (1991). *Collaborating: Finding common ground for multiparty problems.* San Francisco: Jossey-Bass.

Hallinger, P., & Heck, R. (1996). Reassessing the principal's role in school effectiveness: A review of empirical research, 1980-1995. *Educational Administration Quarterly, 32*, 5–44.

Halsted, A., & Schine, J. (1994). Service learning: The promise and the risk. *New England Journal of Public Policy, 10*(1), 251–257.

Heath, S. B., & McLaughlin, M. W. (1987, April). A child resource policy: Moving beyond dependence on school and family. *Phi Delta Kappan, 68*, 576–580.

Heath, S., & McLaughlin, M. (1996). The best of both worlds: Connecting schools and community youth organizations for all-day, all-year learning. In J. Cibulka & W. Kritek (Eds.), *Coordination among schools, families, and communities: Prospects for educational reform* (pp. 50–69). New York: State University of New York Press.

Henderson, A., & Mapp, K. (2002). *A new wave of evidence: The impact of school, family, and community connections on student achievement.* Austin, TX: Southwest Educational Development Laboratory.

Hill, D., & Pope, D. (1995, April). *Establishing a beachhead: Service learning at Stanford.* Paper presented at the annual meeting of the American Educational Research Association, San Francisco, CA.

Hopkins, B., & Wendel, F. (1997). *Creating school-community-business partnerships.* Bloomington, IN: Phi Delta Kappan Educational Foundation.

Jehl, J., & Kirst, M. (1992). Getting ready to provide school-linked services: What schools must do. *Future of Children, 2*, 95–106.

Jones, S., & Hill, K. (2003). Understanding patterns of commitment: Student motivation for community service involvement. *Journal of Higher Education, 74*(5), 516–539.

Kagan, S., Goffin, S., Golub, S., & Pritchard, E. (1995). *Toward systemic reform: Service integration for young children and their families.* Falls Church, VA: National Center for Service Integration.

Keith, N. Z. (1996). Can urban school reform and community development be joined? A potential of community schools. *Education and Urban Society, 28*(2), 237–268.

Kirst, M., & McLaughlin, M (1990). Rethinking policy for children: Implications for educational administration. In B. Mitchell & L. Cunningham (Eds.), *Educational leadership and changing contexts of families, communities, and schools.* Chicago: University of Chicago Press.

Lawson, H., & Hooper-Briar, K. (1994). *Expanding partnerships: Involving colleges and universities in interprofessional collaboration and service integration.* Miami, FL: Danforth Foundation & The Institute for Educational.

Levine, M. (1997). Can professional development schools help us achieve what matters most? *Action in Teacher Education, 19*(2), 63–73.

Longoria, T. Jr., (1998). School politics in Houston: The impact of business involvement. In C. Stone (Ed.), *Changing urban education* (pp.184–198). Lawrence: University Press of Kansas.

Mawhinney, H. B. (1994). *The policy and practice of community enrichment of schools* (Proceedings of the Education and Community Conference, Department of Educational Administration). Toronto: Ontario Institute for Studies in Educational Administration.

McLaughlin, M. (1992). How district communities do and do not foster teacher pride. *Educational Leadership, 50*(1), 33–35.

McLaughlin, M., Irby, M., & Langman, J. (1994). *Urban sanctuaries: Neighborhood organizations in the lives and futures of inner-city youth.* San Francisco: Jossey-Bass.

Melaville, A. (1998). *Learning together: The developing field of school-community initiatives.* Flint, MI: Mott Foundation.

Merz, C., & Furman, G. (1997). *Community and schools: Promise and paradox.* New York: Teachers College Press.

Mickelson, R. (1999). International business machinations: A case study of corporate involvement in local educational reform. *Teachers College Record, 100*(3), 476–512.

Mitchell, A., & Raphael, J. (1999). *Goals 2000: Case studies of promising districts.* Washington, DC: U.S. Department of Education.

Molloy, P., Fleming, G., Rodriguez, C., Saavedra, N., Tucker, B., & Williams, D. Jr., (1995). *Building home, school, community partnerships: The planning phase.* Austin, TX: Southwest Educational Development Laboratory.

Nasworthy, C., & Rood, M. (1990). *Bridging the gap between business and education: Reconciling expectations for student achievement.* Washington, DC: Office of Educational Research and Improvement.

National Center for Education Statistics. (n.d.). Available from http://nces.ed.gov

Nettles, S. M. (1991). Community involvement and disadvantaged students: A review. *Review of Educational Research, 61*(3), 379–406.

Newbold, S. (1996, February). *Connections: Partnerships helping all students succeed.* Paper presented at the Annual Meeting of the Association of Teacher Educators. St. Louis MO.

Newman, L. (1995, April). *School-agency-community partnerships: What is the early impact on students' school performance?* Paper presented at the annual meeting of the American Educational Research Association, San Francisco.

Partnership for Family Involvement in Education. (1999). *Faith communities joining with local communities to support children's learning: Good ideas.* Washington, DC: U.S. Department of Education.

Richmond, G. (1996). University/school partnerships: Bridging the culture gap. *Theory into Practice, 35,* 214–218.

Rinehart, J., Short, P., & Short, R. (1998). Teacher empowerment and principal leadership: Understanding the influence process. *Educational Administration Quarterly, 34,* 630–649.

Rubin, H. (2002). *Collaborative leadership: Developing effective partnerships in communities and schools.* Thousands Oaks, CA: Corwin.

Ruggenberg, J. (1993). *Community service learning: A vital component of secondary school education.* New York: Moral Education Forum.

Salinas, K., & Jansorn, N. (Eds.). (2000). *Promising partnership practices: 2000.* Baltimore, MD: National Network of Partnership Schools, Johns Hopkins University.

Salinas, K., & Jansorn, N. (Eds.). (2001). *Promising partnership practices: 2001.* Baltimore, MD: National Network of Partnership Schools, Johns Hopkins University.

Salinas, K., & Jansorn, N. (Eds.). (2002). *Promising partnership practices: 2002.* Baltimore, MD: National Network of Partnership Schools, Johns Hopkins University.

Salinas, K., & Jansorn, N. (Eds.). (2003). *Promising partnership practices: 2003.* Baltimore, MD: National Network of Partnership Schools, Johns Hopkins University.

Salinas, K., & Jansorn, N. (Eds.). (2004). *Promising partnership practices: 2004.* Baltimore, MD: National Network of Partnership Schools, Johns Hopkins University.

Sanders, M. G. (2001). A study of the role of "community" in comprehensive school, family and community partnership programs. *Elementary School Journal, 102*(1), 19–34.

Sanders, M.G. (in press). Missteps in team leadership: The experiences of six novice teachers in three urban schools. *Urban Education.*

Sanders, M. G., & Epstein, J. L. (2000). Building school, family, and community partnerships in secondary schools. In M. G. Sanders (Ed.), *Schooling students placed at risk: Research, policy, and practice in the education of poor and minority adolescents* (pp. 339–362). Mahwah, NJ: Lawrence Erlbaum.

Sanders, M. G., & Epstein, J. L. (2000). The National Network of Partnership Schools: How research influences educational practice. *Journal of Education for Students Placed At Risk, 5*(1 & 2), 61–76.

Sanders, M. G., & Harvey, A. (2002). Beyond the school walls: A case study of principal leadership for school-community collaboration. *Teachers College Record, 104*(7), 1345–1368.

Sanders, M. G., & Lewis, K. (in press-a). Building bridges toward excellence: Community involvement in high schools. *High School Journal.*

Sanders, M. G., & Lewis, K. (in press-b). Partnerships at an urban high school: Meeting the parent involvement requirements of No Child Left Behind. *E-Journal of Teaching and Learning in Diverse Settings.*

Sandholtz, J., & Finan, E. (1998). Blurring the boundaries to promote school-university partnerships. *Journal of Teacher Education, 49*(1), 13–25.

Shore, R. (1994). *Moving the ladder: Toward a new community vision.* Aspen, CO: Aspen Institute.

Sirotnik, K. A., & Goodlad, J. I. (Eds.). (1988). *School-university partnerships in action: Concepts, cases, and concerns.* New York: Teachers College Press.

Skeele, R., & Daly, J. (1999). Symbiosis: University/school partnerships. *Journal of Interactive Instruction Development, 12*(1), 31–40.

Skrtic, T., & Sailor, W. (1996). School-linked services integration: Crisis and opportunity in the transition to postmodern society. *Remedial and Special Education, 17*(5), 271–283.

Stallings, J. (1995). Ensuring teaching and learning in the 21st century. *Educational Researcher, 24*(6), 4–8.

Stevens, D. (1999). The ideal, real, and surreal in school-university partnerships: Reflections of a boundary spanner. *Teaching and Teacher Education, 15*(3), 287–299.

Stone, C. R. (1995). School/community collaboration: Comparing three initiatives. *Phi Delta Kappan, 76*(10), 794–800.

Stroble, B., & Luka, H. (1999). It's my life, now: The impact of professional development school partnerships on university and school administrators. *Peabody Journal of Education, 74*(3–4), 123–135.

Sullivan, C., & Sugarman, J. (1996). State policies affecting school-linked integrated services. *Remedial and Special Education, 17*(5), 284–292.

Teitel, L. (1994). Can school-university partnerships lead to the simultaneous renewal of schools and teacher education? *Journal of Teacher Education, 45,* 245–252.

Toffler, A., & Toffler, H. (1995). Getting set for the coming millennium. *The Futurist, 29*(2), 10–15.

Tucker, C., Chennault, S., Brady, B., Fraser, K., Gaskin, V., Dunn, C., & Frisby, C. (1995). A parent, community, public schools, and university involved partnership education program to examine and boost academic achievement and adaptive functioning skills of African American students. *Journal of Research and Development in Education, 28*(3), 174–185.

U.S. Department of Education. (1994). *Strong families, strong schools: Building community partnerships for learning.* Washington, DC: Author.

Waddock, S. A. (1995). *Not by schools alone: Sharing responsibility for America's education reform.* Westport, CT: Praeger.

Walsh, M., Andersson, D., & Smyer, M. (1999). A school-community-university partnership. In T. Chibucos & R. Lerner (Eds.), *Serving children and families through community-university partnerships: Success stories* (pp. 183–190). Norwell, MA: Kluwer.

Wynn, J., Costello, J., Halpern, R., & Richman, H. (1994). *Children, families, and communities: A new approach to social services.* Chicago: University of Chicago, Chapin Hall Center for Children.

Wynn, J., Merry, S., & Berg, P. (1995). *Children, families, and communities: Early lessons from a new approach to social services.* Washington, DC: American Youth Policy Forum.

Yonezawa, S., Thornton, T., & Stringfield, S. (1998). *Dunbar-Hopkins Health Partnership Phase II Evaluation: Preliminary Report—Year One.* Baltimore, MD: Center for Social Organization of Schools.

Index

Action Teams for Partnerships (ATPs),
32–33, 52, 56–57
Afterschool activities, 83–84
American Jewish Congress, 23

Bailey, G., 3
Barriers:
    communication challenges, 12
    focus issues, 12–13
    funding, 11–12
    implementation challenges,
        17–18, 21–22
    leadership, 11
    participation challenges, 8–9, 15
    problem-solving skills, 88, 96
    resource identification, 10–11
    time management, 10
    training programs, 21–22
Boyd, W., 9, 20, 21
Business partners, 5–7, 14–16, 49, 68, 92

Career opportunity awareness, 75–76
Cartledge, G., 24–25
Case studies:
    elementary school project, 47–61
    high school project, 62–72
    literacy project, 39–46
Christian Legal Society, 23
Club Mid, 83–84
Combs, L., 3
Communication:
    challenges, 12
    collaborative environments, 43–45
    open communication, 26, 59–60
    oral and written communication
        skills, 81–82
    regularity, 45
    sample letters, 110–111
    two-way communication, 58–60
Community-centered activities, 4, 5, 93
Community Health Fair, 70

Community partnerships:
    complexity, 7–8, 94–95
    contact information handout, 97
    definition, xi
    elementary school project, 48–51
    high school project, 67–71
    importance, 1–3, 91
    influencing factors, 28–38, 98, 108
    obstacles, 8–13, 15, 17–18,
        21–22, 88, 96
    open communication, 26
    partnership activity foci, 3–5, 87, 93
    planning guidelines, 26–27, 105–108
    quality evaluations, 107
    resources, 102–103
    roles and responsibilities, 25–26
    shared vision, 25
    types, 5–7, 14–27, 92
    workshop guidelines and handouts, 85–101
    See also Case studies
Community service involvement, 79–81
Components of success, xii, 28–38
Connections Project, William Woods
        University, 18
Corporate partners. See Business partners
Creative activities:
    afterschool activities, 83–84
    career opportunity awareness, 75–76
    community service involvement, 79–81
    effectiveness evaluations, 107
    landscaping improvements, 79
    math skills, 74–75
    oral and written communication, 81–82
    partner identification process, 105
    quality evaluations, 107
    reading skills, 74, 78
    science skills, 82–83
    state proficiency testing, 76
    students with disabilities, 82
    technology skills, 77
    writing skills, 77

Crowson, R. L., 9, 20, 21
Cultural institutions, 6, 7, 49, 69, 92
Cushing, E., 8, 9

Demographics, 47, 64–65, 112n5
District support, 37–38
Dryfoos, J., 25

Educational institutions, 5, 6, 16–18,
    49, 68, 92
Effective partnership teams, 31–33, 106
Elementary school project:
    background information, 47–48
    community partnerships, 48–51
    demographics, 47
    learning commitment, 51–54
    open communication, 58–60
    principal leadership, 54–57
    school climate, 57–58
Epstein, J. L., 8–9
Evaluation guidelines, 100–101
External support, 36–38

Facilitation, 34
Faith organizations, 6, 7, 22–25, 49, 68, 92
Family-centered activities, 4, 93
First Amendment Center, Vanderbilt
    University, 23
Funding issues, 11–12
Furman, G., 2

Gallagher, R., 22
Gardner, R., III, 24–25
Gemeinschaft values, 2–3
Goal setting, 40, 43
Government agencies, 5, 6, 49, 68, 92

Harvey, Adia, 47
Health care organizations, 5, 6, 49, 68, 92
High-functioning schools, 28–30
High school project:
    background information, 62–65
    community partnerships, 67–71
    demographics, 64–65
    principal leadership, 66
    student involvement, 66–67
Honesty, 59
Hopkins, B., 16
Hundred Book Challenge, 50, 51, 53

Individual volunteers, 6, 7, 49, 69, 92
Intergenerational Writing Project, 81–82
Internship programs, 70–71

Jansorn, N., 73

Keith, N. Z., 3
Kleinhammer-Tramill, J., 22
Knowlton, E., 22
Kohl, E., 8, 9

Landscaping improvements, 79
Language barriers, 12
Leadership:
    collaborative leadership, 43–44
    obstacles, 11
    principals, 33–36, 54–56, 66, 99, 108
Learning environment, 51–54, 57–58
Lewis, Karla, 62
Literacy project case study, 39–46
Local service organizations, 6, 7, 92
Longoria, T., Jr., 15–16

Mahlios, M., 22
Male and Female Youth
    Enhancement Project, 24
Math skills, 74–75
Mawhinney, H. B., 8–9
McLaughlin, M. W., 36
Media organizations, 6, 7, 49, 69, 92
Melaville, A., 16–17
Merz, C., 2
Mickelson, R., 14, 15
Military agencies, 5, 6, 49, 68, 92
Mitchell, A., 36

Nasworthy, C., 16
National Network of Partnership Schools
    (NNPS), xii, 4, 47, 62, 73
National service organizations,
    5–7, 49, 68, 92

Obstacles. *See* Barriers
Oral and written communication, 81–82

Parent involvement, xi, 52–53
    See also Case studies
Partnership for Family Involvement in
    Education, 23
Persistence, 44
Principal leadership, 33–36,
    54–56, 66, 99, 108
Professional development, 18, 85–101
Promising Partnership Practices
    (Salinas & Jansorn), 73

Quilting Project, 79–81

Raphael, J., 36
Reading project. *See* Literacy
    project case study
Reading skills, 74, 78
Recreational institutions, 6, 7, 49, 69, 92
Resources, 102–103
Roles and responsibilities, 25–26
Rood, M., 16
Rubin, H., 44
Ruggenberg, J., 19
Rural High. *See* High school project

Sailor, W., 20
Salinas, K., 73
Schley, G., 24–25
School-centered activities, 4, 93
School climate, 57–58
School-linked service integration, 20–22
Science skills, 82–83
Seidl, B., 24–25
Senior citizens organizations,
    6, 7, 49, 68, 92
Service coordination, 20
Service Learning Center 2000, Stanford
    University, 19–20
Service learning partnerships, 18–20

Service organizations, 5–7
Shared vision, 25
Shore, R., 1–2
Skrtic, T., 20
Social capital, 3
Sports franchises, 6, 49, 69, 92
State proficiency testing, 76
State support, 37
Student-centered activities, 4, 30–31, 93
Students with disabilities, 82

Teamwork, 40–41, 44, 45
Technology skills, 77
Time management, 10

University partnerships. *See* Educational
    institutions
Urban Mission, 70
Utley, C., 24–25

Volunteer organizations, 5–6, 7,
    49, 68, 92

Wendel, F., 16
Woolsey, M., 24–25
Writing skills, 77